Directions 2

Ina Taylor

Published in 2002 by:
Nelson Thornes Ltd
Delta Place
27 Bath Road
CHELTENHAM
GL53 7TH
United Kingdom

02 03 04 05 06 / 10 9 8 7 6 5 4 3 2 1

A catalogue record for this book is available from the British Library

ISBN 0 7487 6388 0

Illustrations by Lisa Berkshire, Angela Lumley, Richard Morris

Picture research by Sue Sharp

Design and page make-up by eMC Design

Printed and bound in Spain by Graficas Estella

Acknowledgements

With thanks to the following for permission to reproduce photographs and other copyright material in this book:

Art Directors & TRIP Photo Library: 5, 25, 26, 56 (all except top middle and bottom right), 58, 63, 86, 93 (all), 94 (both), 102/103, 114, 127; ASAP: 61 (top), 67, 77, 84 (top); Associated Press: 30; Circa Photo Library: 44, 55, 89, 108; Circa Photo Library/ Barrie Searle: 68 (top), 74; Circa Photo Library/ John Smith: 104, 116/117, 124; Corbis/ Tom Nebbia: 36; Corel (NT): 45, 126; Phil Emmett: 100/101; Firepix International: 7; Hulton Archive: 40 (bottom); The Jacob's Bakery Limited: 78; John Birdsall Photography: 34 (portraits); Judges Postcards Ltd, Hastings 01424 420919: 31; Kobal Collection/ Wingnut Films: 48; National Gallery, London: 15, 39; Nelson Thornes/Stuart Boreham: 45; News Team International/ Richard Lea-Hair: 27; PA News: 121; Rex Features/ J.Sutton Hibbert: 21; Sonia Halliday Photographs: 50; Martin Sookias: 61 (bottom), 62 (all), 97; Stone/ John Beatty: 29; Tate Picture Library: 11, 46/47; Ina Taylor: 34 (garden tomb & stone), 40 (top), 41, 42, 43, 49, 52, 53 (all), 65 (inset), 66, 68 (bottom), 80, 82, 83, 84 (bottom), 90, 91, 96, 98, 99, 105, 106, 109, 110, 111, 119, 125, 128; The Trustees for Methodist Church Purposes: 12/13, 19; The Walking Camera: 112/113; John Walmsley: 72; Jerry Wooldridge: 65 (main picture), 122

Every effort has been made to contact copyright holders. The publishers apologise to anyone whose rights have been inadvertently overlooked, and will be happy to rectify any errors or omissions.

Contents

Unit 1

WHAT DOES THE INCARNATION OF JESUS MEAN FOR CHRISTIANS?

Dramatic rescue

Boys save girl from sinking beneath mud

By Simon de Bruxelles

Two boys aged 13 saved an 11-year-old girl from drowning in mud. Alyshia Bennett was seconds from disappearing below the surface when Michael Richards and Merryn Pember came to her rescue.

While Michael held her head and scooped mud away from her mouth Merryn ran to fetch help. They kept her alive for more than 15 minutes until firemen reached her.

Alyshia, who is 4ft tall, became trapped in the mud in a dried-up lake near her home in St Austell, Cornwall, during a blackberry-picking expedition. Her friend, Chloe Foster, ten, also became trapped in the mud but sank only to her waist. After treatment for shock and exposure Alyshia was back at Penrice School yesterday, where she thanked her rescuers by giving them cakes.

She described how she had tried to reach a small island, thinking that the Charlestown Lake had completely dried out. As the ground gave way beneath her feet she carried on running hoping to reach dry land but succeeded only in getting more stuck. The two boys, who were also picking blackberries, thought at first that the girls' screams were a prank and began playing hide-and-seek before realising what had happened.

Alyshia said: 'Michael and Merryn are absolute heroes. They saved my life. If they had not got to me when they did I would have sunk under the sand and mud within two minutes. They tried to pull us out and when they could not, Merryn ran to the nearest house while Michael got on to a log next to me and kept the mud out of my mouth.

He was holding me up and tried pulling my arms. And then he held my chin up with one hand and was scooping the mud away from my mouth so I could breathe, with the other. He was doing that for at least ten minutes before help arrived and all the time I was still sinking and he had to pull me by the hands to try to get me up a bit.'

Terry Nottle, a St Austell fireman, said: 'The two boys saved Alyshia's life. When we arrived she was up to her chin in the mud. We had to lay more branches on it before we could rescue her.'

[from *The Times*, 19 September 2001]

People often get themselves into difficulties. For example, it is not unusual for people to be stranded on a cliff ledge when the tide comes in. You could say it is their fault for being there in the first place, yet most of us would not just walk away and leave them there.

Christians believe that God has the same attitude towards humans. Rather than abandon people to sort out their own mess, God wants to help them out. Sometimes the only way to help others out of their difficulties is to go in and pull them out. The firemen in the picture have done that. Despite the risk to their own lives, they stepped into the flames to rescue the child. Christians believe that in order to rescue humans from the evils they get themselves into, God has to become involved.

This is the problem. How does a divine being, who is so great and powerful, go in among humans, who are so vulnerable and fragile by comparison?

- Would you call the firemen in the photograph on this page heroes, or were they just doing the job they are paid for?

- Who do you think was the hero of the rescue in the newspaper report?

- Role-play an interview with the hero of the newspaper story for Satellite TV News.

- Ask Michael about his thoughts as he struggled to keep mud out of Alyshia's mouth:

  What made him risk his life for a stranger?

  How much danger was he in?

  Was there ever a point at which he thought they might not survive?

- Ask Alyshia about her thoughts and fears: Now that she has had a brush with death, does Alyshia think she will behave any differently?

- 'It is only worth rescuing nice people or young people who have their whole lives to live.' What do you think?

- Should you put your life at risk for your family? Should you put it at risk for strangers or animals? Give reasons for your answers.

ACTIVITY A In groups, design a poster to recruit people for the fire service. Women as well as men can apply. Add something to the poster about the satisfaction of doing a life-saving job.

Superman

Chief problem solver

Some people believed God would send a person to solve their problems. That person would need to be superhuman to carry out such a task. It is difficult to imagine what this person would really be like. Jews use the name *Messiah* for this person.

Messiah means 'anointed one'. The traditional way to create a new king or queen is to anoint, or smear, a small amount of perfumed oil on the person's forehead. Jews therefore thought of the Messiah as a king.

Predictions

There have been many different ideas, gossip and rumours about what the Messiah would be like. Prophets, or messengers from God, arrived at different times in history and told people what the Messiah was going to be like. Isaiah was one such prophet who lived in Israel several hundred years before the birth of Jesus. Some of Isaiah's prophecies are shown on the opposite page along with one from another prophet, called Micah.

The people who walked in darkness have seen a great light.
They lived in a land of shadows, but now light is shining on them.

Isaiah 9:2

A child is born to us!
A son is given to us!
And he will be our ruler.
He will be called, 'Wonderful Counsellor.'
'Mighty God,' 'Eternal Father,' 'Prince of Peace'.
His royal power will continue to grow;
His kingdom will always be at peace.
He will rule as King David's successor, basing his power on right and justice, from now until the end of time.
The Lord Almighty is determined to do all this.

Isaiah 9:6–7

The royal line of David is like a tree that has been cut down; but just as new branches sprout from a stump, so a new king will arise from among David's descendants. The spirit of the Lord will give him wisdom,
And the knowledge and skill to rule his people.
He will know the Lord's will and have reverence for him,
And will find pleasure in obeying him. He will not judge by appearance or hearsay; he will judge the poor fairly and defend the rights of the helpless.

Isaiah 11:1–4

The Lord himself will give you a sign: a young woman who is pregnant will have a son and will name him 'Immanuel'.

Isaiah 7:14

He has chosen me and sent me to bring good news to the poor,
To heal the broken-hearted,
To announce release to captives
And freedom to those in prison.

Isaiah 61:1–2

Bethlehem ... you are one of the smallest towns in Judah, but out of you I will bring a ruler for Israel, whose family line goes back to ancient time.

Micah 6:2

- What does the word Messiah mean?
- Which town did Micah predict the Messiah would come from?

Write the word MESSIAH in a box in the centre of a double page in your exercise book. Choose at least four predictions from the scripture quotations. Write them in your own words as legs of a spider diagram.

- Do you think that we should sort out our own problems rather than expect a greater power to do it for us?
- Name three problems you think we need outside help with solving.

 ACTIVITY A

- List at least five things you would like your own personal helper to be able to do to solve your problems.
- Design your personal helper as a cartoon character. For example, it might have long arms to be able to carry all your school things, eyes on stalks to look round doors and under the bed to find the things you have lost.

Message!

- **What is the dominant colour the artist has used in the picture? What would that symbolise?**

- **How old would you say Mary is in the picture?**

- **The Holy Spirit is traditionally shown as a dove. Find the dove in the picture. What does it seem to be doing?**

LOOKING BACK

Look back to the prophecies of Isaiah on the previous page and copy down the one that best fits the picture.

There is a big splash of red on the right of the picture. It is a piece of embroidered material hanging over a hook. It might be Mary's belt. You notice it because the colour is striking. The artist chose that colour deliberately to prophesy what will happen to Mary's child, Jesus, when he is an adult. What do you think the colour red symbolises?

In Luke's gospel it says that an angel came to Mary before she married Joseph. The angel told her:

Don't be afraid, Mary; God has been gracious to you. You will become pregnant and give birth to a son, and you will name him Jesus. He will be great and will be called the Son of the Most High God.'

Because Mary was still a virgin, she could not understand how she could be pregnant. The angel told her:

The Holy Spirit will come to you, and God's power will rest upon you. For this reason the holy child will be called the Son of God.

If you look carefully at the painting you will see that the artist has tried to show the very moment Mary becomes pregnant by the Holy Spirit. As the angel hands Mary a white lily, the dove passes across in front of her.

The idea of the Messiah being part-human and part-God is called the **incarnation**. Because Christians believe that Jesus had a human mother but the Holy Spirit for a father, they are sure he was the Messiah sent by God.

The angel told Mary to call her child Jesus. The name means 'God saves'. Christians believe Jesus was sent by God to rescue people from the moral mess they had got themselves into. Christians refer to the mess that people get themselves into as sin.

- **Work with a partner:**

  Can you think of any other ways a Messiah could have been derived from both human and God? Why is it important that the Messiah is part-human?

  Is it a greater act of kindness to help someone who has sinned than to help the victim of a natural disaster?

  What kinds of things would you consider to be a sin?

- **Make a list of the different ways we pass messages on to people. How could God send a message to earth today that people would notice?**

- **If you were painting a picture, how else could you show:**

  the idea of innocence

  a message arriving from God.

This is one artist's idea of how God sent his message to earth. Rossetti, who painted the picture, put lots of symbolic ideas into it to show the idea of Jesus as part-man and part-God.

Son of man

This Nativity scene was painted in 1961 by the British artist, Francis Hoyland. He wanted to show several scenes of the nativity story rather like a comic strip. The central picture could be inside any present-day farm building. Jesus has been put up in the hayrack with a lantern above him.

What do you think the artist intended the lantern to represent?

Shepherds receive a message from the angel in the top left picture.

Three wise men back-pack through the woods towards a bright light in the top right picture.

The other three pictures illustrate a story in Matthew's Gospel (2:13–14) where Mary and Joseph had to take their young baby and escape into Egypt. King Herod had ordered the massacre of all baby boys

The Word became a human being and lived among us.

God's message for humanity is sometimes referred to as The Word. The gospel writer, John, uses The Word to represent Jesus and his teaching. This picture tries to show that Jesus led a life as a normal person. He knew what it was like to be human from the inside. Many of us have more respect for leaders if they show that they are like us. For example, if the managing director of a business makes an effort to work on the shop floor, she is more likely to be respected by the workers.

> ● **With a partner examine the picture in detail.**
>
>   **List the things you can see which make this story modern.**
>
>   **Which of these words do you think best describes the painting: helpful, disrespectful, easy to understand?**
>   **Or**
>   **Choose your own words to describe this as a nativity scene.**

> **Do you think images on Christmas cards should make us feel happy? What is the real message of Christmas? Does this apply only to Christians or could it be relevant to people of another or no religion?**

> The Word became a human being and, full of grace and truth, lived among us. We saw his glory, the glory which he received as the Father's only Son.
>
> John 1:14

> **ACTIVITY A** Use pictures taken from magazine adverts to construct a collage of the nativity that aims to show the human side of Jesus, the son of man. Use the words from John's gospel on your poster.

in Bethlehem. The artist visualised this as a modern-day tragedy where a young couple have to grab their baby and run as a vehicle burns in the background. War rages in the bottom picture and a nuclear bomb has exploded in the second picture on the left, leaving a baby dead in the street.

Son of God

Artists and writers have found it hard to show how a baby could be human and yet the son of God at the same time. It is easier to paint or describe the human side of Jesus. This painting by the artist Botticelli attempts to show the nativity scene as something that is beyond human. The picture is called *Mystic Nativity*.

Work with a partner to understand what is going on in the picture:

- **Look at the family. The painter has made them bigger than all the other figures. If Mary stood up her head would hit the roof. What is the artist trying to say by making them that big? Some people think it makes the whole scene more like something in a dream.**

- **If you look carefully at the shoulders of the grey mule, you might be able to make out a cross marked on it. What has the artist reminded people will happen to the baby?**

- **The shepherds are kneeling on the right of the stable where an angel with a pink wing points to the baby. Three wise men to the left of the stable look very similar to the shepherds. Compare them with the wise men and shepherds in the painting by Hoyland on the previous page. What could both artists be trying to say about them by dressing them in the ordinary clothes of the day?**

- **Like Hoyland, Botticelli has painted his idea of hell at the bottom of the picture. Which of the two versions of hell do you find the nastier? Give reasons for your choice.**

LOOKING BACK

- Compare Joseph in this picture with Joseph on the previous page. Why do you think he is shown like this?

- Compare this painting with the previous page. What is Joseph doing in both pictures? What is Mary doing? List three ways in which Botticelli has tried to make his picture 'out of this world'.

Do you think this painting would make a better Christmas card than the previous one? Why?

Jesus was born in the town of Bethlehem in Judaea, during the time when Herod was king. Soon afterwards, some men who studied the stars came from the east to Jerusalem and asked, 'Where is the baby born to be the king of the Jews? We saw his star when it came up in the east, and we have come to worship him'

Matthew 2:1–2

And so they left, and on their way they saw the same star they had seen in the east. When they saw it, how happy they were, what joy was theirs! It went ahead of them until it stopped over the place where the child was. They went into the house, and when they saw the child with his mother, Mary, they knelt down and worshipped him. They brought out their gifts of gold, frankincense, and myrrh, and presented them to him.

Matthew 2:9–10

When the angels went away from them back into heaven, the shepherds said to one another, 'Let's go to Bethlehem and see this thing that has happened, which the Lord has told us.' So they hurried off and found Mary and Joseph and saw the baby lying in the manger. When the shepherds saw him, they told them what the angel had said about the child. All who heard it were amazed at what the shepherds said.

Luke 2:15–18

Of man and of God

He came to what was his own, and his own people did not accept him. But to all who received him, who believed in his name, he gave power to become children of God, who were born, not of blood or of the will of the flesh or of the will of man, but of God.

And the Word became flesh and lived among us, and we have seen his glory, the glory as of a father's only son, full of grace and truth.

(Revised Standard Version)

He came to that which was his own, but his own did not receive him. Yet to all who received him, to those who believed in his name, he gave the right to become children of God – children born not of natural descent, nor of human decision or a human's will, but born of God.

The Word became flesh and lived for a while among us. We have seen his glory, the glory of the one and only Son, who came from the Father, full of grace and truth.

(New International Version)

Read each of the three translations and then choose the one which you think is the easiest to understand. In the first paragraph John is talking about Jesus as a human being. In the second paragraph John is still writing about Jesus but now he is talking of him as God, or a message from God.

Both artists on the previous pages were attempting to show the incarnation of Jesus. *Incarnation* means that God became a person. The middle of the word incarnate (*carn*) you might recognise from the word carnivore, which is a meat eater. *Carn* comes from the Latin word for meat or flesh. The word incarnate means 'to turn into flesh and bone', in other words, to be like a human body.

Trying to explain this idea is no easier than trying to paint it. John, one of the Gospel writers, wrote his account in Greek. There are many English translations and each version tries to make it more understandable. Three different translations are shown in the illustration.

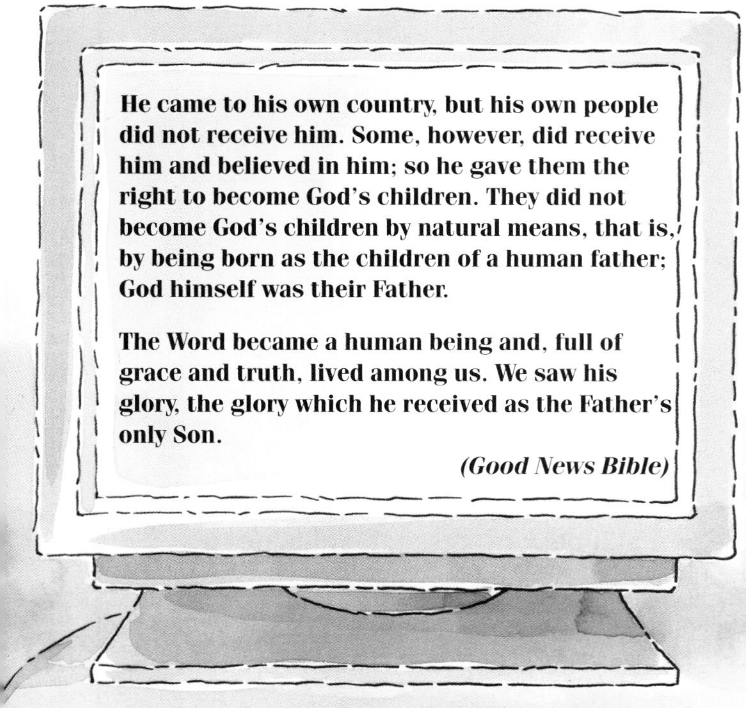

He came to his own country, but his own people did not receive him. Some, however, did receive him and believed in him; so he gave them the right to become God's children. They did not become God's children by natural means, that is, by being born as the children of a human father; God himself was their Father.

The Word became a human being and, full of grace and truth, lived among us. We saw his glory, the glory which he received as the Father's only Son.

(Good News Bible)

ACTIVITY A

Use a clean double page in your exercise book.

● Choose the version of John's Gospel you prefer and copy it onto the right-hand page in your book.

● Using coloured pens draw a line from the correct part of the quotation across to the left-hand page.

● Write the meanings from the panels below into your book. Match it with the correct part of your quotation. You can write the meaning in the same colour, or box it in the same colour to make it clear.

Jesus was God's son

Jesus is one who brings light into the world

Jesus was a real person

Why do you think the Gospel writers continued to emphasise that Mary was a virgin. What were they trying to say about Jesus?

Love in action: Jesus, Lazarus and Martha

A loving action

In John's Gospel much of chapter 11 is devoted to a detailed account of how Jesus raised the man Lazarus from the dead. Jesus knew Lazarus and his two sisters well, so when news came saying Lazarus had died from an illness, Jesus set off to see them. It took a few days to get to the village, by which time Lazarus had been buried for four days.

Lazarus' sister, Martha, understands exactly who Jesus is. She tells him, *'If you had been here Lord, my brother would not have died! But I know that even now God will give you whatever you ask him for.'* She goes on to say, *'I do believe that you are the Messiah, the Son of God, who has to come into the world.'*

Mary, the other sister, also believes that Jesus would not have let their brother die if he had been there when he was ill, but she is too upset to say more.

Jesus saw her weeping, and he saw how the people who were with her were weeping also; his heart was touched, and he was deeply moved. 'Where have you buried him?' he asked them ... Deeply moved once more, Jesus went to the tomb, which was a cave with a stone placed at the entrance. 'Take the stone away!' Jesus ordered ... Jesus said to her, 'Didn't I tell you that you would see God's glory if you believed?' They took the stone away. Jesus looked up and said, 'I thank you, Father, that you listen to me. I know that you always listen to me, but I say this for the sake of the people here, so that they will believe that you sent me.' After he had said this, he called out in a loud voice, 'Lazarus, come out!' He came out, his hands and feet wrapped in grave clothes, and with a cloth round his face. 'Untie him,' Jesus told them, 'and let him go.'

Study the picture:

- **Lazarus starts off in the dark at the bottom of the picture. You can follow him gradually getting up on the right until he stands up. Look at the colour changes.**

- **Where are Lazarus' sisters in this picture?**

- **Who do you think owns the hands? Perhaps the hands are giving a blessing but they also look like a conjurer's hands.**

- **The police hold back the crowds who are still pouring down the hillside to watch.**

- **Some of the crowd have animal heads. The artist said these represent the non-believers.**

LOOKING BACK

- Look back at the written account of the raising of Lazarus and read the complete story in John 11:1-45.

- Jesus did this as an act of love. Which quotes support this statement?

- How does this story show the close relationship Jesus had with God?

- **If you had the chance to ask Martha two questions and then ask Lazarus two, what would they be?**

Love in action: Jesus, Simon and the beggar

Jesus left the synagogue and went to Simon's house. Simon's mother-in-law was sick with a high fever, and they spoke to Jesus about her. He went and stood at her bedside and ordered the fever to leave her. The fever left her, and she got up at once and began to wait on them. After sunset all who had friends who were sick with various diseases brought them to Jesus; he placed his hands on every one of them and healed them all.

Luke 4:38–40

You are a reporter at the scene of mass healing outside Simon's house.

Either:

Write copy for a report in tomorrow's local paper. You will need to include information about who was involved, when and where it took place. Try to include an interview with Simon's mother-in-law. She might tell you how ill she had been and what Jesus actually said to her. Did she think it would be any good? She is likely to tell you about the extraordinary scenes that happened later on in the day.

Or

Role-play an interview for *The Six o'Clock News* with one of those healed. You will need to ask how they got to hear about the activities? What was the atmosphere like? How long did they have to wait? Did it feel strange when it was happening?

ACTIVITY A

Questions	Luke 5:17–26	Luke 8:40–56	Mark 1:40–45
What does Jesus do?			
What makes him do it?			
What does Jesus say about the incident?			
Would you call this an act of love?			
Was anybody watching?			

- Draw a table in your exercise book, or create a spreadsheet on the computer with a column for each story.

- Compare the stories and fill in the results on the table.

As Jesus was coming near Jericho, there was a blind man sitting by the road, begging. When he heard the crowd passing by, he asked, 'What is this?'

'Jesus of Nazareth is passing by,' they told him.

He cried out, 'Jesus! Son of David! Have pity on me!'

The people in front scolded him and told him to be quiet. But he shouted even more loudly, 'Son of David! Take pity on me!'

So Jesus stopped and ordered the blind man to be brought to him. When he came near, Jesus asked him, 'What do you want me to do for you?'

'Sir,' he answered, 'I want to see again!' Jesus said to him, 'Then see! Your faith has made you well.'

At once he was able to see, and he followed Jesus, giving thanks to God. When the crowds saw it, they all praised God.

Luke 18:35–43

- The name that the beggar uses would tell Jesus that the beggar recognised him as the Messiah. Why? What was special about that title?
- What does this tell us about the blind man's understanding of who Jesus is?
- What do people mean when they talk of 'faith healing'?

Complete this sentence in your exercise books. *Jesus showed love towards people by ….* Develop your answer into a paragraph by adding examples. You might also consider how easy it is to show love towards people you already know and like, compared to those you have never met before, especially people who do not look or smell very nice.

- What makes the blind man aware that Jesus is around?
- What title does the beggar use for Jesus?
- If you read the story again carefully you will see that Jesus does not claim to have healed the man. What does he actually say?
- Who does the man thank for his recovery?

Would you say this healing was an act of love, or do you think Jesus had no choice? Give a reason for your answer.

Jesus Christ or Santa Claus?

Most people would say that Santa Claus has nothing to do with Jesus, but there is a connection. Santa comes from the word 'saint' and Claus was once Nicholas. St Nicholas lived a long time ago. It is thought he died around 326 CE. Recently archaeologists have found a tomb on the island of Gemile off Turkey. They are certain that this tomb contained the body of St Nicholas.

It is hard to be sure of the facts about the real St Nicholas as many stories are told about him. He is thought to have been a bishop, who tried to follow Jesus' example in helping people others ignored. It is said that he personally rescued many sailors from drowning when their boats were wrecked on rocks. Other stories tell of him rescuing people who had been wrongfully imprisoned.

It is the story of his anonymous present to three girls that turned him into Santa Claus. Legend has it that the girls' father needed to raise a lot of money to pay their dowries or the marriages would be cancelled. The family was desperate; they had no idea how to raise the money legally. One night three bags of gold were mysteriously thrown through their window. This solved their dowry problem. The money was an anonymous gift from the bishop who felt sorry for the girls.

Bishop Nicholas of Myra is said to have led a very holy life dedicated to God and to helping people. Stories of miracles he performed to heal people have also been passed down through the centuries. After his death he became known as St Nicholas, the patron saint of sailors. His secret presents to the girls led to him becoming the patron saint of children.

In medieval times St Nicholas Eve, on 5 December, was a festival. It was customary to give anonymous gifts. Gradually this tradition merged with the idea of giving Christmas presents to remember the gifts Jesus received from the wise men. St Nicholas became Santa Claus.

- Was Santa Claus ever a real person?
- How was the saint inspired by Jesus?
- Use an atlas or computer program to locate the island of Gemile off the south coast of Turkey .

The Christmas carol, *Good King Wenceslas*, is also believed to have been based on a real person and a true story. The hero of the story was a Christian who was inspired by Jesus' love for others and his teachings. He also put love into action by voluntarily helping others.

Many people give more money to charity at Christmas than at any other time of the year. Carol singing is one obvious way of collecting for charity. Another is buying charity Christmas cards. The charity organisation, *Children in Need,* raises huge sums at Christmas.

Some church groups have a special collection to buy presents for children in hospital or for elderly people on their own. Others give tins of dog and cat food to the rescue kennels, or send money to animal charities to ensure the strays have a good Christmas dinner. This is a way of showing love for part of God's creation.

ACTIVITY A

- Design a survey or questionnaire to find out the following information:

  How important do people think Christmas is?

  How do people celebrate Christmas?

  How do people show concern for others at Christmas in a practical way?

  Does it make any difference to celebrating Christmas whether a person is Christian or not?

- Survey at least ten people from a cross-section of young, middle-aged and older people.

- Based on the results of your survey, write a report entitled 'What Christmas means in the twenty-first century'. Comment on what Christmas gains from being connected to the nativity story. Include your own views in your report.

ACTIVITY A

- Find a copy of the first two verses of the Christmas carol, *Good King Wenceslas*.

- When is St Stephen's Day? Who was St Stephen?

- Look up Wenceslas in an encyclopaedia and note down any historical information about him.

Will you give Mary a bed this Christmas?

TEMPERATURE AT NIGHT	8°C

At 16, Mary ran away from a life of abuse. Today she is homeless. Could you sleep easy this Christmas knowing she was shivering in a bus shelter?

You can help keep Mary, and hundreds of homeless people like her, safe and warm over Christmas. With £25 from you, Crisis can provide a warm bed, hot meals, clean clothes and someone to talk to at one of our shelters.

As the days count down to Christmas, hundreds of vulnerable and isolated people are counting on Crisis. We're counting on **you**. Our services depend on public donations. So please send your **£25** today – in time to help us buy the bedding, food and clothes we need to bring Mary in from the cold.

Yes, I'll keep homeless people warm

Call the number below or complete this coupon and post it to:
Crisis, Room A, FREEPOST, LON17541, London SW1W 0YA.

☐ £15   ☐ **£25**   ☐ £50   ☐ £250

Other £ _____

I enclose a cheque made payable to Crisis UK. **OR** debit my:

☐ Visa   ☐ MasterCard   ☐ Switch†   Other _____

Card no. ☐☐☐☐ ☐☐☐☐ ☐☐☐☐ ☐☐☐☐

† Extra digits of Switch card no. __ / __ / __   Switch issue no. __ / __

Expiry date __ / __   Signature _____

OR please call our freephone donation line

☐ I'd like to know more about helping Crisis long term with a regular gift.

Name (caps) Mr/Mrs/Ms _____

Address _____

_____

_____   Postcode _____

If you do not wish to receive information from other relevant charities, please tick. ☐

CRISIS
WORKING FOR HOMELESS PEOPLE

0800 038 48 38   REF: O

A model has been used and some details changed to protect confidentiality.

Crisis UK trading as Crisis   Registered Charity no 1082947   Company no 4024938

Salvation Army bands often play carols and collect money in shopping centres and town squares at Christmas time.

Salvation Army

This group of Christians are a familiar sight around Christmas. The money they collect is used to help the needy people of society. Members of the Salvation Army work throughout the year, not just at Christmas, to provide food and accommodation for the homeless. By setting up hostels and offering help to those people whom society has rejected, the Salvation Army believe they are putting love into action as Jesus taught.

> I was hungry and you fed me, thirsty and you gave me drink; I was a stranger and you received me in your homes, naked and you clothed me; I was sick and you took care of me, in prison and you visited me ... I tell you, whenever you did this for one of the least important of these brothers of mine, you did it for me!
>
> Matthew 25:35–36, 40

ACTIVITY A

- Find out what charitable activities take place near you at Christmas.
- Design a poster to encourage people to give to one of these good causes at Christmas.
- What can you find out about the Salvation Army's 'soup runs'? How is that connected with Jesus?

Love in action at all times

Christians believe the example and teachings of Jesus give people the best idea of what the love of God is like. They believe that they should copy the actions of Jesus because he freely gave help to anyone in need. The idea of doing something voluntarily might seem strange. Giving up time and not getting paid for it is not easy for most people, yet often we are really grateful when someone helps us.

When you have a long wait for a hospital appointment, or have to take turns to visit a patient, you may be really grateful to buy a cup of tea, a magazine or a bar of chocolate. The person who has served you probably belongs to the hospital League of Friends. These volunteers give up their time to help those who visit the hospital. They may serve in the shop or tea room, or they may direct patients to the right part of the hospital for their treatment. They are not paid for their work; they do it to help others. Any profit the League of Friends' coffee bar or shop makes goes towards buying extra equipment for the hospital.

- Why do Christians particularly believe they should give of their time and money freely?
- With your partner discuss whether you think someone who does a job 'for love not money' does a better job than one who is paid to do the same job.

Some people volunteer to put themselves in the front line when there is trouble. The emergency services in the West Midlands have a group of 30 religious leaders who volunteered to be on hand to help in an emergency. The group includes Christians, Muslims, Sikhs, Hindus and Jews and is called the Birmingham Major Incident Team (Clergy). They work closely with the police, fire and ambulance services. Their leader, the Reverend John Herve said, 'You can do a great deal in an emergency. Priests give people confidence. You're the only people that the wounded and their families can shout at. You're the only person who can hold their hand. The emergency services don't have time. People are glad to find a friendly face. And if they don't want to talk to you, they'll tell you to clear off.' From a completely practical point of view, the minister is able to pass on messages to friends or relatives.

- **Do you think religious people should get involved in major disasters, or would you rather only the emergency services were present? What makes you say that?**

List the reasons the priest in the picture says the Major Incident Team (Clergy) is a good idea.

ACTIVITY **A** Find out why the charity Barnados was set up. What does it do for people today?

A good save

> *For God loved the world so much that he gave his only Son, so that everyone who believes in him may not die but have eternal life. For God did not send his Son into the world to be its judge, but to be its saviour.*
>
> *John 3:16–17*

Christians are convinced that God cares about everything in creation, particularly the human life he made. They also believe that people have destroyed the close relationship that once existed between them and God. Adam, the first man, is said to have disobeyed God and since then people have been growing further and further away from God. By sending Jesus, the Messiah, Christians believe God has offered them the chance to restore their close relationship with him once again. Jesus is their rescuer, the one who will save them from their sins. This will enable people to get closer to God. For this reason Jesus is referred to by Christians as the Saviour.

The idea of Jesus as a saviour is difficult to understand. Even when Jesus explained it to people, many struggled with the concept. In an attempt to make it clearer, Jesus told this story in Luke 15:4–7.

- What does the name 'Jesus' actually mean? Look back to page 10 to remind yourself.
- Look at the quotation from John's Gospel at the top of the page. Why does he say God sent Jesus?
- What do Christians believe Jesus saves people from?

> Suppose one of you has a hundred sheep and loses one of them – what does he do? He leaves the other ninety-nine sheep in the pasture and goes looking for the one that got lost until he finds it. When he finds it, he is so happy that he puts it on his shoulders and carries it back home. Then he calls his friends and neighbours together and says to them, 'I am so happy I found my lost sheep. Let us celebrate!' In the same way, I tell you, there will be more joy in heaven over one sinner who repents than over ninety-nine respectable people who do not need to repent.
>
> *Luke 15:4–7*

ACTIVITY A Jesus told three stories about losing and finding something as a way of helping people to understand God's concern for them.

- In the Bible, read the other two stories in Luke 15:8–10 and Luke 15:11–32.
- Choose one of these stories and rewrite it in a modern setting. You may show the story as a cartoon if you prefer.

Christians often refer to Jesus as 'the lamb of God'. Find out why they use this expression.

Dave grazes over 300 sheep on the Shropshire hills. He could afford to lose the odd lamb without wasting much money, so why does he bother with a scrawny one like this? 'Well the little fellow deserves a sporting chance, doesn't he,' Dave said. 'He has survived so far, I'm not going to give up on him.

If there's a glimmer of life there, I'll do my utmost to give him a go. Of course I miss my bed if I'm out lambing a difficult case on a cold wet night in February. But there it is, isn't it? I get a real buzz a few days later when I see the fellow I've revived, dashing around the field with the others.'

This picture is of Sinterklaas, the Dutch Santa Claus. He looks like a bishop.

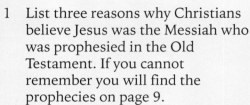

LOOKING BACK

1   List three reasons why Christians believe Jesus was the Messiah who was prophesied in the Old Testament. If you cannot remember you will find the prophecies on page 9.
2   What is the connection with Santa Claus and the fourth century bishop, St Nicholas?
3   In groups of three or four design a poster entitled *Baby with a mission*. You need to show the idea that Jesus, the baby, was sent by God for a purpose. Before you begin working on paper, decide what Jesus was sent to do and what gospel quotation you could use alongside your pictures.
4   Compose a poem around the idea of what Christmas means for a Christian.
5   Write the meaning of each of these words:

incarnation   **prophecy**
                salvation
mystical   **messiah**

GOING FORWARD

1   Consult Oxfam International's website www.Oxfam.org to discover what projects they are currently working on.
2   Find out what practical things the different church groups in your area are doing to put Jesus' message of love for others into action.
3   Design a Christmas card based on John 1:11–14. The quotation appears on pages 16–19.
4   Look up the words of the Christmas carol, *Once in Royal David's City*. List the ideas in this carol that are based on gospel accounts of the birth of Jesus.
5   Look at the website www.nationalgallery.org.uk to see how other artists have painted the nativity scene. Which painting do you like best?

WHAT DOES THE RESURRECTION OF JESUS MEAN FOR CHRISTIANS?

What is happening?

Body vanished! Rumours of man rising from the dead!

The prisoner Jesus was certified dead on Friday afternoon at the scene of his crucifixion. The body was removed from the cross and buried late that afternoon. First reports say the body has gone from the tomb. Security guards deny anyone had access to the site. Stories are coming in that Jesus is alive again.

Following the extraordinary news that has just broken, we have immediately sent out our four investigators. Their reports appear here and on the next page. We have also set up an incident centre to examine the evidence thoroughly. Your help is urgently needed!

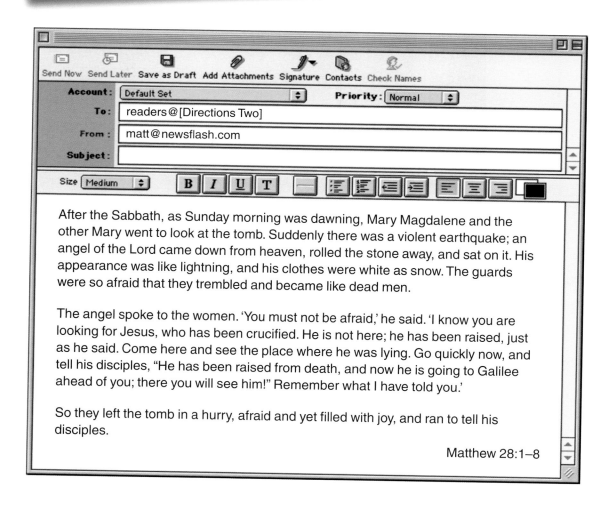

Send Now Send Later Save as Draft Add Attachments Signature Contacts Check Names

Account: Default Set   **Priority:** Normal

To: readers@[Directions Two]

From: matt@newsflash.com

Subject:

Size Medium   B I U T

After the Sabbath, as Sunday morning was dawning, Mary Magdalene and the other Mary went to look at the tomb. Suddenly there was a violent earthquake; an angel of the Lord came down from heaven, rolled the stone away, and sat on it. His appearance was like lightning, and his clothes were white as snow. The guards were so afraid that they trembled and became like dead men.

The angel spoke to the women. 'You must not be afraid,' he said. 'I know you are looking for Jesus, who has been crucified. He is not here; he has been raised, just as he said. Come here and see the place where he was lying. Go quickly now, and tell his disciples, "He has been raised from death, and now he is going to Galilee ahead of you; there you will see him!" Remember what I have told you.'

So they left the tomb in a hurry, afraid and yet filled with joy, and ran to tell his disciples.

Matthew 28:1–8

Report

from Mark

After the Sabbath was over, Mary Magdalene, Mary the mother of James and Salome bought spices to go and anoint the body of Jesus. Very early on Sunday morning, at sunrise, they went to the tomb. On the way they said to one another, 'Who will roll away the stone for us from the entrance to the tomb?' (It was a very large stone.) Then they looked up and saw that the stone had already been rolled back. So they entered the tomb, where they saw a young man sitting on the right, wearing a white robe – and they were alarmed.

'Don't be alarmed,' he said. 'I know you are looking for Jesus of Nazareth, who was crucified. He is not here – he has been raised! Look, here is the place where they put him. Now go and give this message to his disciples, including Peter; "He is going to Galilee ahead of you; there you will see him, just as he told you."'

So they went out and ran from the tomb, distressed and terrified. They said nothing to anyone, because they were afraid.

Mark 16:1–8

Compare the reporters' stories to discover the facts of this case. Two reporters' stories appear on these pages and two more are on the following pages 34–35. List what each reporter says about the day, the time, the people present and any other things he mentions. You could use a computer spreadsheet or a grid similar to the one below to list the facts. Add any further categories to the left-hand column you think necessary. Some, like earthquakes, may only appear in one box, so put a dash in the other boxes.

	Matthew	Mark	Luke	John
Day				
Time				
Women mentioned				
Men mentioned				
Place				
Unnatural occurrences				

Collecting the evidence

Garden Tomb

Joanna

Mary Magdalene

Rolled back stone

Security Guard

Mary Mother of James

Simon Peter

Salome

Look closely at the information we have received from our four reporters about the activities of each suspect on the board. List the details we have about each one. Take special note of any inconsistencies in the reporters' stories.

Luke's fax is coming in with the following story.

From: Luke

Very early on Sunday morning the women went to the tomb, carrying the spices they had prepared. They found the stone rolled away from the entrance to the tomb, so they went in; but they did not find the body of the Lord Jesus. They stood there puzzled about this, when suddenly two men in bright shining clothes stood by them. Full of fear, the women bowed down to the ground, as the men said to them, 'Why are you looking among the dead for one who is alive? He is not here; he has been raised. Remember what he said to you while he was in Galilee: "The Son of Man must be handed over to sinful men, be crucified, and three days later rise to life."'

Then the women remembered his words, returned from the tomb, and told all these things to the eleven disciples and all the rest. The women were Mary Magdalene, Joanna, and Mary, the mother of James; they and the other women with them told these things to the apostles.

But the apostles thought that what the women said was nonsense, and they did not believe them. But Peter got up and ran to the tomb; he bent down and saw the linen wrappings but nothing else. Then he went back home amazed at what had happened.

Luke 24:1–12

John's report arrived by post.

Early on Sunday morning, while it was still dark, Mary Magdalene went to the tomb and saw that the stone had been taken away from the entrance. She went running to Simon Peter and the other disciple, whom Jesus loved, and told them, 'They have taken the Lord from the tomb, and we don't know where they have put him!'

Then Peter and the other disciples went to the tomb. The two of them were running, but the other disciple ran faster than Peter and reached the tomb first. He bent over and saw the linen wrappings, but he did not go in. Behind him came Simon Peter, and he went straight into the tomb. He saw the linen wrappings lying there and the cloth which had been round Jesus' head. It was not lying with the linen wrappings but was rolled up by itself. Then the other disciple, who had reached the tomb first, also went in; he saw and believed. (They still did not understand the scripture which said that he must rise from death.) Then the disciples went back home.

John 20:1–10

Some late material from John.

Mary stood crying outside the tomb. While she was still crying, she bent over and looked in the tomb and saw two angels there dressed in white, sitting where the body of Jesus had been, one at the head and the other at the feet. 'Woman, why are you crying?' they asked her.

She answered, 'They have taken my Lord away, and I do not know where they have put him!'

Then she turned round and saw Jesus standing there; but she did not know that it was Jesus. 'Woman, why are you crying?' Jesus asked her. 'Who is it that you are looking for?'

She thought he was the gardener, so she said to him, 'If you took him away, sir, tell me where you have put him, and I will go and get him.'

Jesus said to her, 'Mary!'

She turned towards him and said in Hebrew, 'Rabboni!' (This means 'Teacher'.)

'Do not hold on to me,' Jesus told her, 'because I have not yet gone back up to the Father. But go to my brothers and tell them that I am returning to him who is my Father, and their Father, my God and their God.'

So Mary Magdalene went and told the disciples that she had seen the Lord and related to them what he had told her.

John 20:11–18

Weighing up the evidence

The investigating officer has asked for clarification of the following points. Please research and submit the results as soon as possible.

- Our reporter, Mark, says some women watched the crucifixion. Please find out who they were. Consult Mark 15:40–41. Are there any similarities with the women at the tomb?

- There are rumours that Jesus was not actually dead when he was taken down from the cross. Please check the details of his injuries in Matthew 27:27–35 and John 19:31–37.

- Check the burial details in Mark 15:42–47 in case there has been a mistake in identifying the tomb.

- Why were women walking around with spices? Find out what they were going to do with them.

The security guard who was in charge of the team of three men on tomb duty over the weekend is in deep trouble. He has been accused of professional negligence and is in danger of losing not only his job, but possibly his life, if he is found guilty. He knows that his team did their duty perfectly. It was not their fault that this man's body vanished. This was not a normal situation and no human being could have stopped it.

- Write a report which the security guard can send to his boss about this incident.

The case

As a class you are going to take part in a court case to decide if Jesus' body vanished miraculously or whether there was a perfectly natural explanation for what happened.

You will need people for the following parts:

- judge
- 12 members of the jury
- at least one security guard
- all the witnesses whose pictures appeared on the incident board on page 34

- court ushers to call the correct witnesses
- someone to lead the case for the miraculous disappearance of Jesus
- someone to lead the case for a natural explanation for the vanishing body
- you may also like to call Joseph of Arimathea as a witness or someone else you feel might know something.

At the end of the proceedings the jury must decide on their verdict. While they are out of the room discussing it, everyone else in the class has the chance to vote on the outcome of this case.

Christians and the resurrection

Did it really happen that way?

NO

Christians believe that Jesus rose from the dead, but not all Christians are convinced that it was a body which came to life again. They say the stories in the four Gospels were not intended to be taken literally, that they were written to explain the difficult idea of a spiritual resurrection. Although Jesus' body was dead, his ideas, his spirit and his work lived on. Christians believe that the spirit of Jesus is still active in the world today, giving help to those who need it.

One leading member of the Church of England, the former Bishop of Durham, controversially said the resurrection story should not to be taken literally. He said Jesus' resurrection was more than a juggling trick with bones. His views caused a national outcry and were not shared by the majority of Christians.

YES

A large number of Christians believe the account of Jesus' body returning to life is a factual account of what happened. To support their argument they point to the fact that quite a few people saw Jesus after his resurrection at different times and in different places. It is not likely that they were all deceived. If the disciples were trying to deceive others, it is difficult to see what they achieved. They never became rich and famous in their lifetimes. They lived hard lives away from family and friends, continually on the move and preaching. All told the same story even when threatened with violence, and many were killed for their beliefs. Today, almost two thousand years after the event, the number of people who believe the resurrection really happened runs into millions.

The point of it all

Christians believe that the resurrection of Jesus means there is life after death. During his lifetime Jesus told his followers that death was not the end. For those who believed in him, he said, there would be eternal life.

> For what my Father wants is that all who see the Son and believe in him should have eternal life. And I will raise them to life on the last day.
>
> John 6:40

> I am the resurrection and I am the life. Whoever believes in me will live, even though he dies: and whoever lives and believes in me will never die.
>
> John 11:25–26

> When I go, you will not be left all alone; I will come back to you. In a little while the world will see me no more, but you will see me; and because I live you also will live. When that day comes, you will know that I am in my Father and that you are in me, just as I am in you.
>
> John 14:18–20

> For God loved the world so much that he gave his only Son, so that everyone who believes in him may not die but have eternal life.
>
> John 3:16

This scene was painted around 1515 by the artist, Titian. He shows the moment when Mary Magdalene suddenly recognises the risen Jesus and reaches out to touch him. Jesus is pulling back from her. He has the white grave cloth wrapped round him. Can you see the nail holes in his feet? Mary has a jar of something in her hand. What do you think it is? (The extracts on pages 33 and 35 will remind you and help you to understand the scene the artist is trying to show.) Look at how the artist has tried to convey the idea that Jesus brings life with him. Compare the ground at his feet with the ground at Mary's feet. Look at the lush green background with a lake and sheep grazing behind Jesus. Behind Mary there are dry rocks.

- **What is your opinion of Jesus' Resurrection story? Why do you say that?**

- **Why do you think the words from John 11:25–26 are used in a Christian funeral service?**

- **Why do Christians believe in the Resurrection?**

- **What does a bodily resurrection mean?**

- **How is a spiritual resurrection different?**

A new life

Coventry Cathedral is made up of two buildings. The one on the left is an old ruin. It is all that remains after German bombs landed on it during the Second World War. The ruin represents death and destruction. On the right is the modern cathedral that has been built; it represents new life. The two buildings are linked by a huge porch which rises above the ruin and stands for the resurrection. A large cross hangs proudly at the top of the porch. The statue on the wall of the new cathedral shows St Michael triumphing over the devil. Why do you think they have chosen to put the statue on the new side of the cathedral?

Death and destruction

On the night of 14 November 1940, the city of Coventry was bombed heavily by the Luftwaffe, the German air force. This resulted in the death of 568 people and many more were injured. The next morning the city was in ruins and its 600-year-old cathedral a smouldering wreck. Only the outer walls and tower remained.

Many people were in tears and full of hatred for the Germans. Richard Howard from the cathedral said they should not waste time on hate but plan to rebuild the cathedral as soon as possible to show they believed in the future.

This old photograph shows the scene inside Coventry Cathedral immediately after the bombing. Can you see the cross-shaped roof timbers?

The charred cross

On the morning after the bombing, the cathedral workmen looked at the wreckage in despair. One of them, Jock Forbes, noticed two of the big rafters from the cathedral roof had crashed down and landed in a cross shape. He pulled them out, bound them together and set up a makeshift altar in the ruin. A local vicar picked up three blackened nails from the rubble, wound some wire around them and made a cross of nails.

The people of Coventry could not start rebuilding their cathedral for another 15 years because they had to replace their homes first. The Second World War was fought until 1945 and many places suffered huge destruction and loss of life. The British suffered, but so did the Germans, who endured terrible losses at the hands of the British. One of their greatest tragedies was the bombing of the city of Dresden by the RAF on 13 February 1945. 25 000 people were killed in one night and Dresden Cathedral was burned to the ground.

The charred cross made from those burned roof timbers stands on the altar today. It is a powerful symbol of suffering. Notice the words that have been written behind the altar. This is what Jesus said when he was dying on the cross. Read the whole quotation in Luke 23:34. Who do you think the people of Coventry are asking God to forgive?

The Cathedral brought back to life

In 1956 Queen Elizabeth II came to Coventry and laid the first stone of the new cathedral, returning in 1962 to open the finished building. The architect who won the competition to design a new cathedral was Sir Basil Spence. He said, *'I was deeply moved. I saw the old cathedral as standing clearly for the Sacrifice, one side of the Christian Faith, and I knew my task was to design a new one which would stand for the Triumph of the Resurrection. In these few moments the idea of the design was planted. In essence it has never changed.'*

Many other countries were inspired by the determination of Christians in Coventry to rebuild their cathedral. Help and donations came from all over the world, including Germany.

> **What happened to the original cathedral in Coventry?**

> - **Why would a cross made of nails be particularly appropriate to the crucifixion story?**
> - **What is the connection between Coventry Cathedral and the story of the Resurrection?**

> **Find out more about the bombing of Coventry on 14 November 1940 and the bombing of Dresden on 13 February 1945? What has happened since in Dresden?**

Peace and reconciliation

International Ministry of Reconciliation and Forgiveness, Coventry Cathedral

A stunning new cathedral was not the only good thing to come out of the tragedy of that November night in 1940. The Provost, one of the leaders of the Cathedral, went to Germany soon after the war to make peace with the people. Many British people hated the Germans, preferring revenge to reconciliation. The Provost believed in following Jesus, who even as he was dying on the cross, asked God to forgive the people who were killing him. The Provost took a cross made from the nails of the old cathedral with him. He said that he wanted *'to say and do something about the situation of division and hatred which accompanied the destruction of the city and the cathedral'*.

His visit was the beginning of Coventry's work for international peace. A centre was established and has grown continually. Today this peace movement has set up many little groups they call A Community of the Cross of Nails. They work for peace in places like Croatia and Northern Ireland. In Israel the community is made up of Jews, Christians and Muslims who have combined to try and bring peace to the area. Today there are over 20 communities working towards reconciliation, justice and peace.

All this good work came out of pain, suffering and death. Christians believe this is putting Jesus' message into practice. For them the resurrection is not a supernatural story that happened two thousand years ago; it is a life-giving message for today.

> **Peace is what I leave with you; it is my own peace that I give you.**
>
> John 14:27

The International Peace Centre has offices in the crypt under the old cathedral. The movement has now grown so much that it now has larger offices in the city as well.

This bronze statue is called Reconciliation. It was placed in the ruins of Coventry Cathedral in 1999 and an exact copy was given to the Peace Garden in Hiroshima in Japan. It marked 50 years since the end of the Second World War and was a token of reconciliation with the people of Japan. On the base it says, 'remind us that in the face of destructive forces human dignity and love will triumph over disaster and bring nations together in respect and peace.'

- Why did the Provost at Coventry want to go to Germany after the Second World War?
- What did many people think about this?
- Why would Christians support him?

Why do you think Hiroshima was chosen as the site for the other *Reconciliation* statue?

- Read more about Coventry's International Ministry on www.coventrycathedral.org/international. Select information from this website to produce a press release that could be issued by Coventry's International Ministry to tell people about their work.
- What symbol of peace and reconciliation could you design for the world today? It does not have to be especially Christian, but it does need to have meaning.

The meaning of Easter

One guidebook to Coventry Cathedral says visitors should start in the old ruined Cathedral then walk through into the new Cathedral. They would feel what it was like to be moving from Good Friday with death and suffering through to the light and joy of Easter Sunday and the Resurrection.

For Christians Easter Sunday is the most important festival of the year. Many people assume that Christmas is the biggest celebration of all because it is a time when everyone spends a lot and eats too much. Christians would agree that celebrating the birth of a baby, especially when that baby is the Son of God, is important, but without Jesus' death and resurrection Christianity would be meaningless.

Christians believe that, by his Resurrection, Jesus shows that he has conquered sin and death. It means that from now on everybody has the chance to go to God when their physical body dies. The idea of new life is central to Easter celebrations. Eggs are symbols of new life because they have the potential to hatch into chicks. Other symbols of new life include the bunnies and flowers that appear on cards.

In some churches it is traditional to create a small Easter garden. List the things you can see in this garden that remind Christians of the accounts of the Resurrection given on pages 32–35.

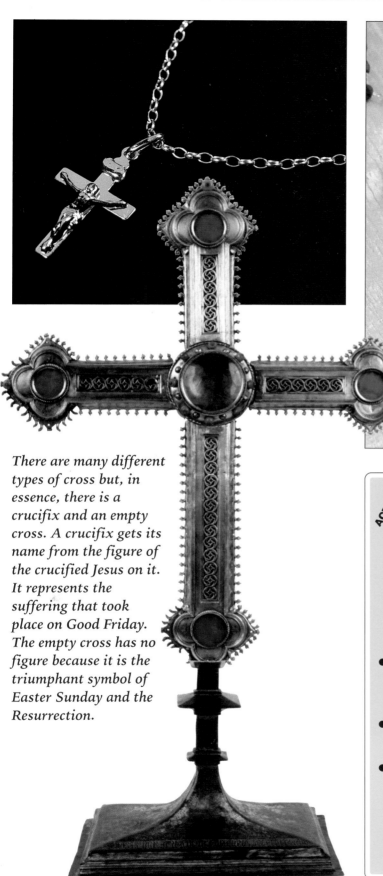

There are many different types of cross but, in essence, there is a crucifix and an empty cross. A crucifix gets its name from the figure of the crucified Jesus on it. It represents the suffering that took place on Good Friday. The empty cross has no figure because it is the triumphant symbol of Easter Sunday and the Resurrection.

ACTIVITY A

- Use the National Gallery's website www.nationalgallery.org.uk to look at their collection of paintings on-line. Artists who have painted Resurrection scenes include Rembrandt, Hans Memling, Mantegna and Piero della Francesca, among many others.

- List four pictures (with the artists' names) that show the idea of the Resurrection.

- Against each write how the artist has shown the idea of rebirth and new life.

- Which of the pictures do you prefer? Why? You might also consider the Resurrection scene at the start of this unit on page 31. It is a tapestry which hangs behind the altar in Coventry Cathedral.

Life after death

This painting is one artist's idea of the Resurrection. Stanley Spencer wanted to show the Resurrection as a modern event. He set it in the churchyard of his own village. Jesus is shown as a mother who is cuddling babies in the Church porch. God stands behind with arms that come over her. Gravestones pop off and people climb out of their graves. Some are making their way over to the pleasure boats in the top left-hand corner of the picture to sail off to heaven. Others look as if they have just woken up! Spencer, the painter, said, 'No one is in any hurry … Here and there things slowly move off but in the main they resurrect to such a state of joy that they are content … In this life we experience a kind of Resurrection when we arrive at a state of awareness, a state of being in love, and at such times we like to do again what we have done many times in the past, because now we do it anew in Heaven'.

- With a partner look closely at the picture and decide what you think is going on in different parts of the scene.

- How do you react to the picture? Do you think it is fun? Is it disrespectful? Is it helpful?

- Compare this painting with the one on page 39. Which do you prefer?

Ghosts and angels

Nobody likes to talk about death, yet most of us enjoy a good ghost story. If you asked people whether they believe in life after death, what proportion would you expect to say yes? If you asked them whether they believe in ghosts, would you get the same result? Do you think more people will say yes?

After death

Christians believe that after we die we will have to answer to God for the way we behaved on earth.

Those who have led a good life will be united with God in heaven. Those who are truly sorry for the things they did wrong will be forgiven by God because Jesus paid the price for people's sins by dying on the cross.

Some Christians believe that just as Jesus was resurrected bodily, they too will be resurrected in their body after they die. Others, who believe that Jesus' Resurrection was a spiritual one, also think their resurrection will be spiritual. Their soul will go to heaven, not the body they have worn on earth.

A ghost is generally accepted as being the spirit of a dead person who is visible to the living. People's ideas of what ghosts might look like vary from cuddly cartoon characters to scary spooks in horror films. Belief in ghosts is not restricted to religious people.

Christians and atheists claim to have seen ghosts. Equally, there are Christians, atheists and members of other religions who think ghosts do not exist at all. Find out why some people claim ghosts exist. What do you think?

This very modern statue is called Angel of the North and is near Gateshead. It is huge and has the wingspan of a jumbo jet. Some people love the statue but others hate it because it is not everyone's idea of what an angel is like. Christians and Muslims believe in the existence of angels as messengers from God.

Angels differ from ghosts in that they have never been human. A few people believe that when people die, they become angels and flutter around God. Angels tend to look after the living and bring messages to them from God.

- Do you think that God communicates differently with people in the twenty-first century?
- What kinds of modern communication systems might be used?

ACTIVITY A

In groups of three or four, organise a survey of people's opinions on this subject. Plan a series of questions you can ask people about their thoughts and beliefs on what happens after death. Find out people's beliefs about angels as well. Be sensitive about the way in which you ask the questions.

- Try to phrase the questions so it is easy for you to collect the data.
- Survey a wide range of people so you can get religious answers and non-religious answers. You also want a cross-section of ages and gender.
- Record your data on a spreadsheet.
- Either mount the spreadsheet on a poster that gives additional information about the subject, or report your group's findings back to the class and compare your questions and results with others.

Where do people find hope?

This brightly coloured stained-glass window in the new part of Coventry Cathedral is said to represent the light of the risen life of Jesus breaking into our human life. It is in the baptistry area of the Cathedral where babies are christened to welcome them into Christianity. What does the theme of the window have to do with baptism?

Some people find hope through religious belief. Christians believe that the life of Jesus has given them a hope for the future. By giving up his life voluntarily, Christians are sure Jesus has overcome the fear of death for all who believe in him. They believe that there is a life after this one and the way we live now will affect what happens to us next. Some religions believe this will take the form of judgement after we die. Other religions like Hinduism, Buddhism and Sikhism believe our behaviour here will determine the way in which we are reborn into this life.

Never give up hope

John McCarthy, a journalist for a television news company, was kidnapped in Beirut and held captive for five years. Later he described how he and another captive, Brian Keenan, tried to remain hopeful despite the filthy conditions and brutal treatment they often received from their guards.

In the wall by my mattress I found a small hole drilled through to the outside. I couldn't imagine why it was there, but it gave me a view across a wide space to yet more blocks of flats and beyond them to the mountains. Judging by the movements of the sun we knew we were looking across Beirut to the Christian sector. Brian, who knew the city far better than I, felt sure we weren't in the southern suburbs, the stronghold of the Hezbollah and other extreme Shia groups, but in the heart of the city, close to the famous shopping street of Hamra. This, too, encouraged me to think we'd be off home soon, as did finding a small stash of dollars under the carpet.

Describe another situation where someone finds hope from something simple.

You may like to read the whole book, *Some Other Rainbow* by John McCarthy and Jill Morrell. It tells of John's capture and five-year imprisonment. His friend Jill also writes of the campaign she started to get him released.

I needed to take whatever good, hopeful impulses I could from the situation, the sound of children's voices, light from the moon and sun coming in around the metal black-out – simple wonders – all encouraged me to hang on. Even the sound of battle helped – it made me realise yet again that there were people worse off than me. As I listened to the fighting I imagined families hugging together as they sheltered in the basement praying to escape for another night, determined to pick up their lives as soon as the shelling ceased. Sadly, Sayeed [the guard who had previously beaten them up] decided to seal up the gaps round the window. We argued that we needed the fresh air. He just laughed. As normal the job was slightly botched so we got a little light through to remind us that the sun still shone and my little spyhole remained intact.

From *Some Other Rainbow*, by John McCarthy and Jill Morrell

- List the ordinary things that gave John McCarthy hope.
- In what way did these things seem special to him when most people would never have noticed them?

ACTIVITY A
- Design a window, a banner, a sculpture or a garden that will convey a similar idea to the baptistry window. You might prefer to think of it in terms of hope breaking despair.
- Find out more about either the Hindu, Buddhist or Sikh beliefs about rebirth and the afterlife. You will need to discover what karma is.

1   Write an account of the resurrection story in your own words.
2   Write a paragraph explaining why Christians believe in the resurrection of Jesus.
3   Use the information about Coventry Cathedral in this unit to produce a guide to the cathedral for a young person. You could make a mini-guide from a folded A4 sheet.
4   Design a book cover for a Christian publication entitled *The Resurrection believe it or not*.

5   In pairs make a poster about Easter. Combine the original Easter story with the way it is celebrated by Christians today.

1   In groups of three or four, either create a model out of recycled materials that represents Peace, or make something beautiful out of rubbish.
2   Research Coventry Cathedral further in books or on the Internet. These sites might help you:
    www.cwn.org.uk/heritageday
    www.exponent.co.uk/peter/covcath
    www.coventrycathedral.org
3   Look at the interactive Easter Garden on www.culham.ac.uk/EasterGarden to learn more about Joseph of Arimathea.

4   Research further information about the Christian International Peace Service on www.cips.org.uk Find out about the time they received a Coventry Cross of Nails.
5   Look at the 'In Memoriam' column in your local newspaper and write down the different ways in which people express their hope and belief in an after-life.

This statue from Coventry Cathedral is called Christ Crucified. It is made out of recycled metal from a wrecked car.

Unit 3 ➤ WHAT DOES IT MEAN TO BE JEWISH?

The logo

Signs, symbols and logos

We identify signs and symbols regularly in daily life. They are an extremely useful form of shorthand. They are eye-catching and save us time from having to read a lengthier explanation. Look at the collection of symbols above. If you had to explain exactly what one of them meant to somebody from another culture, it would take you several minutes. Signs contain a great deal of information for those who know how to interpret them.

Difference between a sign and a symbol

A sign often contains basic information which nobody feels much emotion about. Road signs and washing labels are fairly neutral but when a symbol represents the Nazi party, or witchcraft, emotions can be involved.

All religions use symbols because they are a convenient way of conveying lots of information. For members of that religion a symbol can stir deep emotions and enable the believer to think about complex ideas they find difficult to express. Think about the emotions and ideas, both happy and sad, that a cross symbol will create in a Christian. The same shape might be totally neutral to another person.

This stained-glass window from a synagogue contains several important symbols of Judaism, the Jewish religion. The seven-branch candlestick is called a menorah and is the oldest symbol of Judaism. It reminds Jews of the six days of creation and the seventh day when God rested. The six-point Star of David is the best known symbol of Judaism. Palm leaves, olive branches, grapes and vines can also be used.

This is the flag of Israel with the Star of David in the centre. David was one of the greatest kings in Jewish history. He is famous for the battle with the giant, Goliath, which marked the beginning of a very successful career as a military leader. It is thought that David had a design like this six-pointed star on his shield. For this reason the symbol is called Magen (or shield) of David.

- With a partner go through the symbols on these pages and identify them. Make a list of what each one means.

- Are there any symbols here that would make you very wary if you saw them on a package?

ACTIVITY A

- Draw three more symbols that you think would make people react in a particular way. Ask people sitting near you to identify them.

- Does it help you to feel you belong if you wear a logo of your group?

Different faces of Judaism

Small but influential

Judaism is the smallest of the six main world religions. If you look at the diagram you can probably estimate the world population of Jews. Despite their small numbers, the Jewish community has made a large contribution to western culture. The collage of images contains some of the different faces of Judaism and a search of the American and British entertainment industry will reveal just how many Jewish film stars and singers there are.

In the beginning

The history of the Jewish people fills the first part of the Bible called the Old Testament by Christians. It names Abraham as the founder of the religion because he insisted his tribe worship only one God. Jews believe that God spoke directly to Abraham and struck a bargain with him. This bargain is known as the Covenant.

God promised:

- to look after the Jews
- to make them his chosen people
- to give them a land of their own

The Jews promised:

- to love God
- to obey his commandments

A land of their own?

God directed Abraham to take his tribe to the country we now call Israel and this became their homeland. The tribes already living there did not agree that the Jews could occupy the country and battles began. Battles continue today over the rightful claim to the land. Many Jews have left Israel and now live all over the world.

Who is Jewish?

Traditional Jews accept a person as Jewish only if the mother was Jewish. Some modern groups of Jews will accept a person as Jewish if either parent was Jewish or that person had a Jewish upbringing. It is possible to convert to Judaism, although this is uncommon.

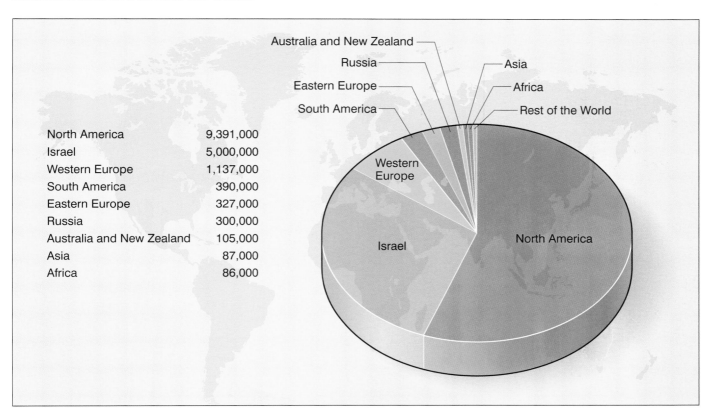

North America	9,391,000
Israel	5,000,000
Western Europe	1,137,000
South America	390,000
Eastern Europe	327,000
Russia	300,000
Australia and New Zealand	105,000
Asia	87,000
Africa	86,000

This shows where Jewish people can be found living today.

Look at the diagram and the website www.bbc.co.uk/religion/religions/judaism.

- Work out the size of the Jewish population of Israel and compare it with the number of Jews in the rest of the world.

- Which European country has the largest Jewish population?

- What is the approximate Jewish population of the UK?

- Who do Jews look to as the founder of their religion?

- What was the Covenant?

Six million Jews were massacred in the twentieth century, that is a third of the world population of Jews. What name is given to this horrific event? Who was responsible for this and why did they do it?

Concepts of God

'When I put on my tallit, that's this shawl I wear every day for morning prayer, I feel the love of God is wrapped all around me. As a Jew I believe strongly that God does love everyone he created. He listens to our prayers and takes care of us.'

Lord, you have examined me and you know me.
You know everything I do;
From far away you understand all my thoughts.
You see me, whether I am working or resting;
You know all my actions.
Even before I speak,
You already know what I will say.
You are all round me on every side;
You protect me with your power.
Your knowledge of me is too deep;
It is beyond my understanding.

Psalm 139:1–6

Read this extract from Psalm 139 and list at least three things it says about the things God knows about everybody.

Sometimes you may see the name of God written like this with the centre letter missing. This is because some Jews feel it is wrong to write such a holy name on paper which can easily be ripped up or thrown away. This would be disrespectful, they believe. To prevent any disrespect to God, the name may appear as G-D.

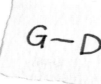

When Moses asks God what name to use for him when he is telling the Jews about God, Moses is told this: '*I am who I am. This is what you must say to them: "The one who is called I AM has sent me to you"*.' (Exodus 3:14).

Some Jews refer to God by the Hebrew word Hashem which means 'The Name'. They believe this is more respectful than saying God's name.

Read this part of the Amidah prayer which is said daily by Jews and list at least three things it is saying God can do.

You, O Lord, are the endless power that renews life beyond death;
You are the greatness that saves.
You care for the living with love.
You renew life beyond death with unending mercy. You support the falling, and heal the sick.
You free prisoners, and keep faith with those who sleep in the dust.
Who can perform such mighty deeds, and who can compare with You,
A king who brings death and life and renews salvation?
You are faithful to renew life beyond death.
Blessed are You Lord, who renews life beyond death.

Amidah prayer

Read this passage. Write down what it says God did.

In the beginning, when God created the universe, the earth was formless and desolate. The raging ocean that covered everything was engulfed in total darkness, and the power of God was moving over the water.

Genesis 1: 1–2

- Use the points you have extracted from the passages on these pages and the information you got from the picture, to write a paragraph explaining what Jews think about God and the power of God.

- In pairs, discuss whether you think words or names can be powerful. Why do people get upset when someone calls them names? Why does swearing upset people? They are only words. Does it have any effect on you if someone swears at you in a foreign language you do not understand?

- These may be useful words to use when describing God:

  Omnipotent = all powerful

  Omnipresent = always there, everywhere

  Omniscient = knows everything

Read the scripture quotations and select a quotation to go with each of these words.

A personal relationship with God

One of the important Jewish beliefs about God is that despite being so great, God has a personal relationship with every part of his creation. Jews believe that it is possible for them to have a personal relationship with God. They can communicate directly with God. They do not need to go through anyone else nor do they need to say any set prayers. People can speak directly to God using whatever words they like. Some prefer to put themselves in a position where they can feel they are quietly in the presence of God. For them words are unnecessary. They believe God knows exactly what is in their minds even before they do.

> God has indeed heard me: he has listened to my prayer. I praise God because he did not reject my prayer or keep back his constant love from me.
> Psalm 66:19–20

> God created human beings, making them to be like himself.
> Genesis 2:27

> O Lord your greatness is seen in all the world!
> Psalm 8:1

> Where could I go to escape from you? Where could I get away from your presence?
> If I went up to heaven, you would be there;
> If I lay down in the world of the dead, you would be there.
> If I flew away beyond the east or lived in the farthest place in the west, you would be there to lead me, you would be there to help me.
> I could ask the darkness to hide me or the light round me to turn into night,
> But even darkness is not dark for you,
> And the night is as bright as the day.
> Darkness and light are the same to you.
> Psalm 139:7–12

> The Lord is my protector;
> He is my strong fortress.
> My God is my protection, and with him I am safe.
> He protects me like a shield;
> He defends me and keeps me safe.
> I call to the Lord, and he saves me from my enemies.
> Psalm 18:2–6

Some people prefer to worship alongside others. It gives them a strong sense of community and they find it easier to get into the right frame of mind.

Where do you go when you want to get away and think? Many people like to be in their own room, by themselves, surrounded by familiar objects.

Describe your ideal quiet place. Where do you like to go to get away and think things over?
Describe the atmosphere that suits you best. Is it out in the open, with space and light all around? Or do you prefer somewhere tucked away and dark?

ACTIVITY **A** Draw two spider diagrams, one with the words *private worship* in the centre, and the other with *public worship* in the centre. Use one colour for the spider's legs to show the advantages of each form of worship and another colour to show the disadvantages.

In the right frame of mind

Do the clothes you wear make any difference to how you feel?

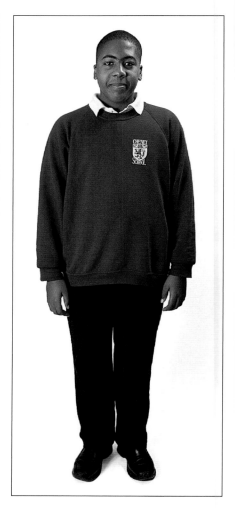

Consider the following points with a partner and report back your opinions to the class.

- Does it make it easier to settle down and work in school if you are wearing a uniform?

- What is the difference in the way the person in the picture feels when he is dressed in his supporter's gear?

- What difference would it make if you had to wear school uniform to a disco?

- Why do people like to wear similar clothes to their friends?

- What does it say about you if you follow fashion? What does it say about you if you ignore fashion?

- Would you rather police and paramedics were allowed to wear what they liked? Do you think it helps them to behave as we expect if they are in uniform?

- Do you think putting on certain clothes can affect your mood?

Kippur – by putting a cap on his head, a Jew is reminded that God is above him.

Tefillin – these leather boxes with straps remind a Jew that he must keep God's commandments. You can read about the tefillin in more detail on page 65.

Tallit – this shawl is worn for morning prayer and reminds a Jew of the love of God wrapped around him.

Jewish men put on special items of clothing before they begin morning prayer. Each has a meaning and helps to focus a worshipper's mind on God.

- Look at the religious garments worn by Sikhs on page 93.

- List the different ways in which religious people are reminded of God's presence.

- What other religious clothing is worn by other religions to help them focus on worship?

Shema

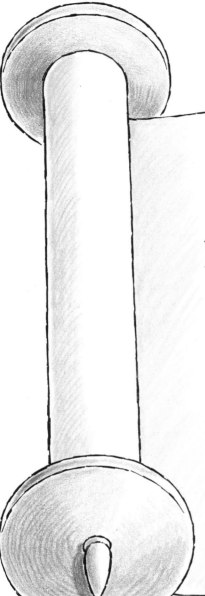

Hear, O Israel: The Lord our God the Lord is one.

You shall love the Lord your God **with all your heart, with all your soul, and with all your might. And these words which I command you this day shall be in your heart. You will** teach them to your children, **and you shall** speak of them when you sit at home, **and** when you go on a journey, when you lie down, **and** when you rise up. **And you shall bind them for** a sign on your hand, **and they shall be as** ornaments between your eyes. **And you shall** write them on the door-posts of your house, **and upon your gates.**

Deuteronomy 6:4–9

This is the most important prayer in Judaism. It is called the Shema because that is the first word of the prayer in the Hebrew language. The first line sums up the Jewish belief that there is only one God and God is at the heart of every part of Jewish life.

- Read the prayer.
- In your exercise book list all the points that have been highlighted in the text.
- Against each one write down what a Jewish person could do to obey these commands. (The pictures as well as the text here will help you.)

וידבר יהוה אל משה לאמר קדש לי כל בכור פטר כל רחם בבני ישראל באדם ובבהמה לי הוא ויאמר משה אל העם זכור את היום הזה אשר יצאתם ממצרים מבית עבדים כי בחזק יד הוציא יהוה אתכם מזה ולא יאכל חמץ היום אתם יצאים בחדש האביב והיה כי יביאך יהוה אל ארץ הכנעני והחתי והאמרי והחוי והיבוסי אשר נשבע לאבתיך לתת לך ארץ זבת חלב ודבש ועבדת את העבדה הזאת בחדש הזה שבעת ימים תאכל מצת וביום השביעי חג ליהוה מצות יאכל את שבעת הימים ולא יראה לך חמץ ולא יראה לך שאר בכל גבלך והגדת לבנך ביום ההוא לאמר בעבור זה עשה יהוה לי בצאתי ממצרים והיה לך לאות על ידך ולזכרון בין עיניך למען תהיה תורת יהוה בפיך כי ביד חזקה הוצאך יהוה ממצרים ושמרת את החקה הזאת למועדה מימים ימימה

The tefillin are worn on the forehead and on the arm to obey the Shema. These leather boxes contain the words of the Shema written on parchment and tucked inside. You can see the Shema written in Hebrew at the top of the picture.

This little box, called a mezuzah case, is nailed to a front door. The mezuzah is a small parchment with the words of the Shema handwritten on it. Read the words of the Shema again to find out why a mezuzah case is nailed to the front door.

Read the Shema again carefully and write down exactly what time of the day a Jew is commanded to recite this prayer.

- **Jews are commanded to teach the Shema to their children. What would be the advantage of doing that?**
- **Islam also has a statement that sums up Muslim belief. What is it? What similarities does the Islamic Declaration of Faith have with the Shema?**

If you want to keep something or someone in mind during the day, what ways would you use?

ACTIVITY A Use the website www.jewish.co.uk or www.jewishnet.co.uk to learn more about the Shema, the mezuzah and tefillin.

Let us meet

Synagogue comes from the Greek word *synago* meaning 'meeting' or 'get-together'. The synagogue is a place where Jews meet to worship, to learn more about Judaism and to enjoy a social life. Judaism is a way of life as much as a religion.

Because people meet outside as well as inside, a synagogue can be in the open air. The most famous open-air synagogue is the Western Wall in Jerusalem, in Israel, but it is more usual to have a building as a synagogue. This offers privacy to concentrate on God without being distracted. You do not have to worry about the weather either.

 On the title page of this unit (page 53) there were photographs of the outside of several synagogues. What do they have in common? Unlike a church or mosque, there is no traditional design for the outside of a synagogue so they vary considerably. It is possible some will display symbols of the religion.

Can you remember the main symbols of Judaism?

Are any of these symbols visible in the pictures on page 53?

This section of wall was once part of the original Temple in Jerusalem over 2000 years ago. Today it is an open-air synagogue. Jews come here to pray. This is the women's side for prayer.

- How does the word 'synagogue' get its name?
- What is the name of the most famous outdoor synagogue?
- Why do some people prefer to worship God alongside other people rather than on their own?

Dear Sir or Madam

Our synagogue committee was very impressed with the meeting we had with your agency. New Millennium Designs is obviously a very forward-looking company with just the sort of exciting ideas we are looking for.

Please would you submit one or two possible designs for the front entrance of our new synagogue? It could be just the doorway or the whole of the front elevation of the building. Our community has a lot of young people and so we want something very exciting and new, but with a few traditional elements if possible. Please send in your proposed design with notes attached as soon as possible.

Yours faithfully

Jeremy Greenbaum

Some people find great spiritual strength in being with others of a similar faith. This group of Jewish people are worshipping together in the synagogue.

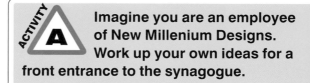

ACTIVITY A

Imagine you are an employee of New Millenium Designs. Work up your own ideas for a front entrance to the synagogue.

In the sanctuary

The ark is open to show the holy scrolls inside but it would not be left like this. Jews treat the scrolls with great respect because they believe the scrolls contain the words of God. The scrolls are decorated with beautiful material and silver ornaments to show they are precious to the Jewish people.

- Above the ark hangs a lamp that never goes out. In Hebrew it is called ner tamid, meaning everlasting light. It shows that God is always there. Traditionally these lamps were oil, but today many are electric.

- At the top stand the Ten Commandments written in Hebrew. Sometimes they are carved on two pieces of stone just like the ones God gave to Moses. Other synagogues have them carved, or written, on the wall above the ark. Often only the opening words of each Commandment appear in Hebrew because the whole Commandment would take up a lot of space.

- The ark containing the scrolls is behind the curtain. The door of the ark is closed and the curtain drawn across the ark to show the scrolls are being safely cared for.

- To reach the ark you walk up steps, showing that the word of God is above people.

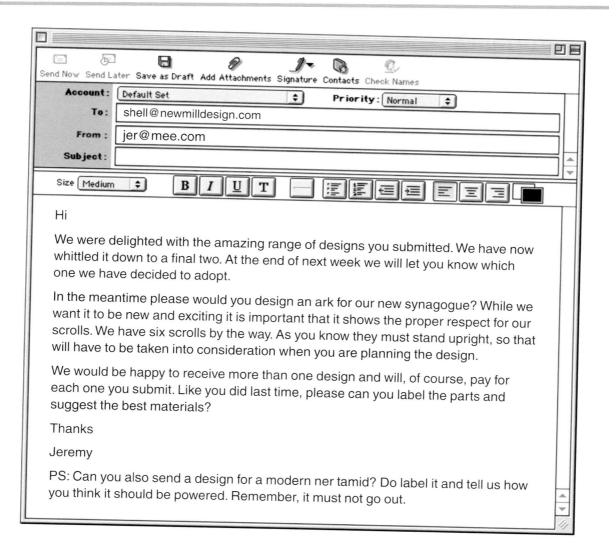

Send Now · Send Later · Save as Draft · Add Attachments · Signature · Contacts · Check Names

Account: Default Set   **Priority:** Normal

To: shell@newmilldesign.com

From: jer@mee.com

Subject:

Size Medium   B I U T

Hi

We were delighted with the amazing range of designs you submitted. We have now whittled it down to a final two. At the end of next week we will let you know which one we have decided to adopt.

In the meantime please would you design an ark for our new synagogue? While we want it to be new and exciting it is important that it shows the proper respect for our scrolls. We have six scrolls by the way. As you know they must stand upright, so that will have to be taken into consideration when you are planning the design.

We would be happy to receive more than one design and will, of course, pay for each one you submit. Like you did last time, please can you label the parts and suggest the best materials?

Thanks

Jeremy

PS: Can you also send a design for a modern ner tamid? Do label it and tell us how you think it should be powered. Remember, it must not go out.

- **Which is the holiest part of the sanctuary?**

- **Name two things Jews do to show their respect for this part of the synagogue.**

- **What is ner tamid and why is it called that?**

- **How did the Jews get their Ten Commandments?**

- **The Ten Commandments have to be put above the ark but how would you do this to fit in with the idea of your modern synagogue? Find the Ten Commandments in English in a Bible and copy them down. They can be found in Exodus 20.**

- **Do you like the idea of treating something as precious? Or would you rather everything was treated the same?**

ACTIVITY A — **Design the material that Jeremy requests.**

Worship

Ark – this most important part of the synagogue faces Jerusalem, so in Britain it is at the east end of the building. More details of this area of the sanctuary appear on page 68.

Bimah – this is a raised platform in the centre of the synagogue containing a reading desk. The scroll is placed here when it is brought from the ark to be read during a service. The bimah is raised up so everyone can hear the reading and people are reminded that the word of God is above them. The cantor, who leads the worship in the synagogue, also stands in the bimah to conduct the service.

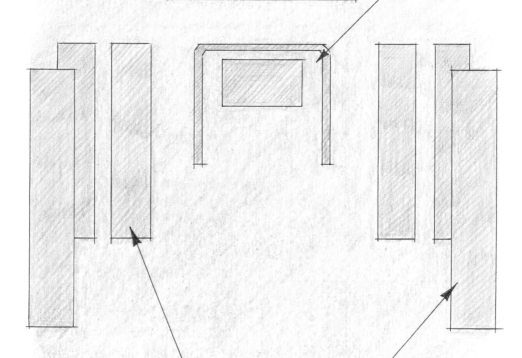

Seats for men – in a traditional synagogue men lead the worship and are the only ones permitted to read from the scrolls. They sit at ground level, below the ark, and face across the synagogue towards the bimah.

Balcony for women – in a traditional synagogue men and women sit apart for worship so they do not distract each other. Children can sit with either parent. Women usually sit up in a balcony, or in a special area at the back of the synagogue.

Orthodox and Progressive

Even among a group of Jewish people you would find differences in the way they worship and the way they interpret some aspects of the religion. Similarly, in a family, members will have different ways of dealing with issues, yet they all belong together and care for each other.

In Judaism there are those who think it is important to keep to tradition or the religion will lose its way. These Jews, called Orthodox, say that because the traditional ways were given to them by Moses, who learned them from God, it means they must be correct and should be followed.

Progressive Jews, who are smaller in number in Britain, believe that the religion must adapt as the society changes.

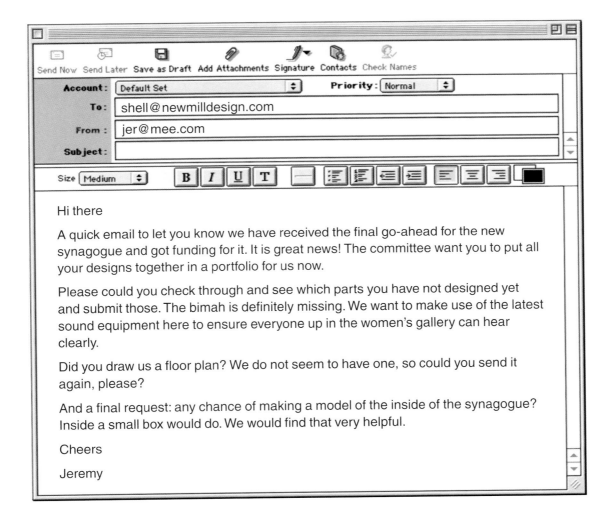

Send Now Send Later Save as Draft Add Attachments Signature Contacts Check Names

Account: Default Set   **Priority:** Normal

To: shell@newmilldesign.com

From: jer@mee.com

Subject:

Size Medium   B I U T

Hi there

A quick email to let you know we have received the final go-ahead for the new synagogue and got funding for it. It is great news! The committee want you to put all your designs together in a portfolio for us now.

Please could you check through and see which parts you have not designed yet and submit those. The bimah is definitely missing. We want to make use of the latest sound equipment here to ensure everyone up in the women's gallery can hear clearly.

Did you draw us a floor plan? We do not seem to have one, so could you send it again, please?

And a final request: any chance of making a model of the inside of the synagogue? Inside a small box would do. We would find that very helpful.

Cheers

Jeremy

Do you think a religion should move with the times? What advantages would there be? What problems might it create?

ACTIVITY A Complete the design that Jeremy asked for. If you are feeling really bold, you could make a model of the synagogue.

The scriptures

With a partner consider the following: If you belong to a club does it help to have some rules? Do you think it makes a group stronger to know who belongs and who does not? Would it weaken the group if anyone could wander in and out and do as they liked? Are there any safety issues that ought to be covered by rules?

Who is in charge?

Most people think it helps to have somebody in overall charge of a group. It might be uncomfortable if you are one of the people who is told what to do, but without anyone in charge everything could be in chaos. Nothing constructive will get done. Have you noticed that even when you do not actually appoint a leader in a group, one often emerges to take charge.

At different times in the Jews' past, a leader has emerged to calm down the warring tribes and take them forward. In addition to having a leader, it is helpful to have an authority that can be consulted on the correct procedures.

Torah means 'the law' in Hebrew. It is the name of the most important part of the Jewish scriptures because Jews believe the words were given to them by God in Hebrew. The Torah contains the rules God wants them to keep. By handing them down the generations with great care and reading them in their original language, Jews believe they are able to keep as close as possible to the way God intended them to lead their lives.

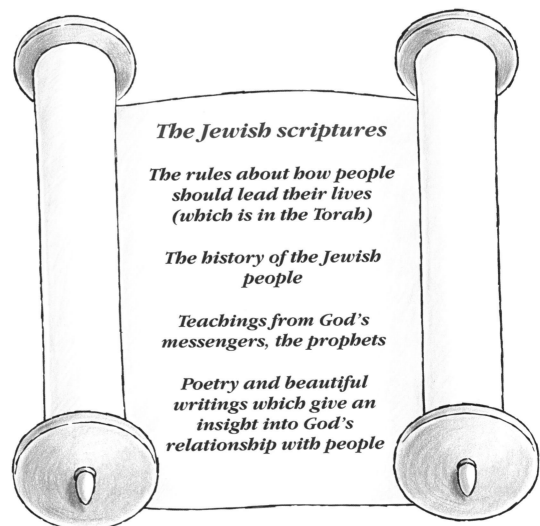

The Jewish scriptures

The rules about how people should lead their lives (which is in the Torah)

The history of the Jewish people

Teachings from God's messengers, the prophets

Poetry and beautiful writings which give an insight into God's relationship with people

- What advantage could there be in knowing about what happened in your childhood or in your family's past?
- Why do the Jews look to the Torah for the answer when trying to decide what to do?
- Why do you think Jews do not like to use translations of their scriptures? With a partner consider the advantages and disadvantages of using any book in translation.

Why do the Jews use the name Torah for part of their scriptures?

As a class, discuss this question: 'No rules – does that mean freedom or bedlam?'

How the scriptures are used

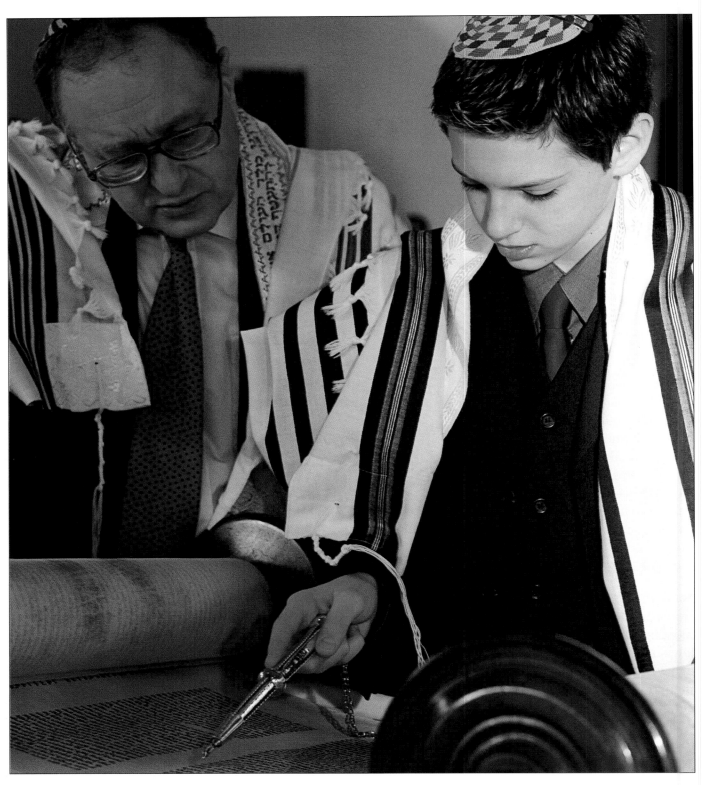

Jews do not want the words in the Torah to ever get smudged or damaged. If this happens then inaccuracies would creep in and God's laws would no longer be clear. To prevent smudging and to show how much they respect the words of God, Jews use a metal pointer, called a yad, to follow the Hebrew words as they read.

Check the rules

Jews use the Torah as a textbook for good behaviour. The rabbis, who have studied the Jewish laws, use the Torah to advise people on all aspects of daily life. It might be what sort of food is safe to eat, who you can marry or whether it is acceptable to have an abortion. Jews believe that the Torah contains rules about everything, though some may need to be interpreted to suit life in the twenty-first century. The word for a rule in Hebrew is *mitzvah*; *mitzvot* is the plural.

Public ceremonies

As in most religions, the Jewish scriptures have an important part in synagogue worship. A portion of the Torah is read aloud every week, so that by the end of the year, the whole Torah has been read.

There are other parts of the Jewish scriptures that are read aloud especially at festival times because their theme is closely connected with the festival.

When a boy reaches the age of 13 he is expected to take responsibility for his religious life. To mark this passage into adult responsibility, he is called up in the synagogue to read aloud from the Torah, like the boy in the picture.

Passages from the scriptures are read or recited at important stages in life, like birth, marriage and death ceremonies.

Private use

Passages from the scriptures are used in some prayers that are said at home. Some Jews find it helpful in their daily life to spend time reading and thinking about a particular passage of scripture on their own, or in a small study group. They feel this helps them to understand how God wanted them to live their lives.

Is it possible to set rules which will apply for all time? What would be the argument against doing this? Why would some people say it is possible?

With a partner think of four modern-day dilemmas that would not be mentioned in the Torah because the technology did not exist. Share them with the class. As a group, work out what sort of advice might cover this topic. Could it be to do with stealing? Or is it a matter of life and death?

 ACTIVITY A Design a poster on a double page in your exercise book. Put the words **TORAH – The Ultimate Authority** in the centre and use words or small sketches to show the way Jews use their scriptures.

Keeping the mitzvot

The Shabbat mitzvot

The Torah tells Jews more than once that they must set aside one day of the week as a holy day. The fourth of the Ten Commandments given by God to Moses is shown in the illustration.

Jews interpret this commandment, or mitzvah, to mean that they should not do any chores on Shabbat, the Sabbath day. This is a day for the family and study of the scriptures. Many Jewish families attend synagogue together on Saturday morning to hear the Torah read and spend the rest of the day visiting family and friends or at home. Some more religious Jewish families will take the opportunity for extra Torah study in the afternoon.

OBSERVE THE SABBATH AND KEEP IT HOLY. YOU HAVE SIX DAYS IN WHICH TO DO YOUR WORK, BUT THE SEVENTH DAY IS A DAY OF REST DEDICATED TO ME. ON THAT DAY NO ONE IS TO WORK – NEITHER YOU, YOUR CHILDREN, YOUR SLAVES, YOUR ANIMALS, NOR THE FOREIGNERS WHO LIVE IN YOUR COUNTRY.

EXODUS 20:8-11

Jews place great emphasis on the importance of family life and Shabbat is a time for family.

No chores means no cooking, no housework and no homework. The Torah lists 39 precise jobs that cannot be done on Shabbat, but Jews understand from the Ten Commandments that no work should take place. All housework, food preparation and cooking must be finished before Shabbat begins so that the day is a rest for everyone. Because one of the 39 things forbidden on Shabbat is lighting a fire, modern Orthodox Jews do not switch on an electrical appliance. Electricity involves a spark and that, they say, is making fire. Modern Jewish families do make use of timing devices to operate lights and other electrical appliances, provided these are set beforehand.

- How would you feel about having one day a week set aside as being different? Are there advantages in that or would you rather every day of the week was the same – get up, go to work, earn money and spend it?

- With a partner think about the mitzvah that prohibits the use of electricity on Shabbat. Work out what differences it would make to your normal day. Remember that you can set timers.

- Is there any value in spending time with your family? It might be holidays, mealtimes, Christmas or family parties. Would you want to include the wider family in any activities, relatives like grandparents, aunts and cousins?

Keeping kosher

You may not have noticed that some everyday foods you eat are marked so that a Jewish person will know whether the food obeys the mitzvot. This chocolate biscuit has a symbol in the bottom right-hand corner. K = kosher, D = dairy and LBD = is the London Bet Din which is the Jewish court of rabbis who have inspected the production of this biscuit and are satisfied it obeys the rules in the Torah.

CLUB Chocolate combines thick milk chocolate with a smooth chocolate flavoured cream and a crunchy biscuit

INGREDIENTS: Milk Chocolate (52%), Wheat Flour, Vegetable and Hydrogenated Vegetable Oil, Sugar, Glucose Syrup, Rolled Oats, Raising Agents (Ammonium Bicarbonate, Sodium Bicarbonate, Disodium Diphosphate), Fat Reduced Cocoa Powder, Salt, Flavouring, Emulsifier: Soya Lecithins.

The Jacob's Bakery Limited, P.O. Box 14, Liverpool, L9 7JX, U.K. Made in England

A company of the DANONE GROUP

All affixed Trademarks belong to, or are used under licence by, subsidiaries of the DANONE GROUP.

Suitable for Vegetarians

5013 7978

You are what you eat!

Food is something that interests most people and occupies a reasonable amount of our time every day. If you have to cook and prepare the food as well, then it takes even longer. Eating is, of course, a pleasure but it is also vital for our survival. We take care about what we eat because the food is used by our bodies to make new body cells and becomes part of us.

The Torah contains many mitzvot to help Jews lead the sort of lives God requires. One key area that is mentioned is food. This may not be so surprising when you think how worried we get when there is a 'food scare' in the newspapers or on television. BSE, E. coli, salmonella and listeria have all been in the news in the past few years. Most are connected with the meat we eat; in the case of listeria, it concerned dairy products. These are the two main food areas that the Torah sets out rules about.

- With a partner try and work out some of the food rules that exist in our society. You could look at the way raw meats and cooked meats are stored on the deli counter of a supermarket. How must people who serve meat be dressed? Look at where dairy products like cheese and milk are stored in the supermarket. Are there any similarities with the Jewish kosher rules?

- If a Jewish person had a beef sandwich at lunch-time, would they be able to eat the biscuit in the picture? What would bread have to be spread with to keep it kosher? Explain your reasons.

- McDonald's have opened in Israel and do serve kosher food. What sort of changes would they have needed to make to their usual menu?

- Read Leviticus 11 and see if you can work out what the rules are for eating:

  animals

  birds

  fish.

- Explain what is meant by 'you should not mix a live and dead element'. How do Jews put this mitzvah into practice?

It is kosher

Chapter 11 of Leviticus, in the Torah, gives clear guidance about what sort of food is good and safe to eat. These rules are known as the Kosher Laws and were established when the Jews were a nomadic desert tribe with limited hygiene and few safe methods of food preservation.

Three basic kosher rules

- blood should be removed from meat. This is because blood represents life. An animal is slaughtered by cutting its throat. The carcass is hung up to drain and joints of meat are soaked in salt water to extract the blood. After rinsing, the meat can be cooked and eaten.

- only meat from permitted animals can be eaten (these are listed in Leviticus 11)

- meat and milk must not be eaten in the same meal. The Torah says three times 'you must not boil a kid in its mother's milk.' Rabbis have interpreted this to mean meat must not be eaten with dairy products. In other words, you should not mix a live and a dead element. This mitzvah includes milk in any form like yoghurt, butter or cream. No product, like a cake, that uses milk in its production can be eaten in a meat meal either. Several hours must lapse between eating meat and then a milk product.

ACTIVITY A Design a poster for the school kitchens to help the staff understand the kosher rules.

Synagogue community life

Because the word synagogue means 'meeting place', most synagogues have several rooms in addition to the sanctuary where worship takes place. This is because the synagogue is at the heart of a Jewish community. Most members of an Orthodox Jewish family are likely to visit the synagogue occasionally during the week for social events, in addition to worship.

In the photograph, the building on the left contains the sanctuary downstairs and a smaller ark and worship area upstairs. This can be used for smaller congregations mid-week. Upstairs also houses the rabbi's study and offices for other synagogue officials because this synagogue is at the hub of a large Jewish community. On that floor there is also a library and if you look at the poster you can see what types of books the library contains.

This modern synagogue is part of a large complex. You can see the front of this synagogue in one of the photographs on page 53.

The large building to the right of the entrance into the car park also belongs to the synagogue and is mainly concerned with the social life of the community.

Downstairs there is a large banqueting hall and kitchens, as well as toilet and cloakroom facilities. This makes it convenient for members of the synagogue community to hold parties and other family functions. Upstairs are rooms that can be used for smaller meetings with facilities for children to play as well as learn about their religion.

Worship

The synagogue is the heart of Jewish community worship. Morning prayers will be said in the synagogue every day. Families try to attend synagogue on Shabbat, the Jewish holy day which begins at Friday sunset and lasts until Saturday sunset. There is a Friday evening service at the synagogue to welcome in Shabbat. Often it is the male members of the family who attend this service, while the women welcome in Shabbat at home. On Saturday morning all the family try to attend synagogue together. The Amidah prayer is recited (extracts from this prayer appear on page 59). After this the ark is opened and one of the Torah scrolls is carried in procession round the synagogue to the bimah. The congregation listen to the reading of the portion of scripture for the week. This is the main focus of the service and the rabbi may explain points from this reading in his sermon.

CRAWSHAW ROAD SYNAGOGUE LIBRARY

Everyone is welcome to borrow books from the library. Please write your name, the title and today's date in the book on the desk. Then tick it off and put the date when you return it.

We have got a rich resource for our community with a wide range of books, including novels, poetry, non-fiction, history, cookery, books on the Hebrew language, children's books and humour (those Jewish jokes...).

The library is all catalogued on the computer so it is easy for you to check whether we've got what you are looking for.

- If you have got books of Jewish interest which you could spare, please consider giving them to the library.
- If you have recently read a book which you think others might enjoy, please drop a note of it in the Suggestions Box.
- It has been traditional for some people to give a donation to the library fund as a way of marking a special family event. Please consider it.

Any suggestions about the library will be happily received by Jenny Saunders.

What do you think a family would gain by making an effort to worship together once a week?

- Look at the list of synagogue activities on page 85 and write down what other things might happen there on Shabbat.

- Using the list of activities on page 85 explain what some Jewish families might do on Friday evening to welcome in Shabbat at the synagogue.

ACTIVITY A Research more information about Shabbat worship on one of these websites or in the school library.
www.jewish.co.uk
www.theresite.org.uk

Life-cycle events at the synagogue

Starting out at the synagogue

The synagogue is at the heart of Jewish life. Here Jews celebrate some of the important stages of their lives with family and friends. Some parents like to bring their new baby to the synagogue for a ceremony of thanksgiving during the Saturday morning service. In front of family, friends and members of the community, the baby is given his or her name.

Coming of age

The next important milestone in the life of a Jewish person is the age at which they take on their religious responsibilities for themselves. At the age of 13 for a boy, and 12 for a girl, a young person is considered mature enough to understand their religious duties. Both boys and girls take extra lessons in aspects of Judaism, the scriptures and the duties of a Jewish man or woman. In Orthodox Judaism it is only the boy who stands up in the synagogue and reads aloud his passage from the scrolls. This can be seen on page 74. In Progressive Judaism a girl would also read the scriptures aloud in the synagogue. Afterwards, family and friends enjoy a party which might be in the synagogue hall or at another location.

This boy was a keen Manchester City supporter, so he requested his party be at Maine Road.

Marrying at the synagogue

Jewish couples like their marriage to be witnessed by family, friends and God. In the picture the couple are standing in the synagogue in front of the ark (with the doors closed) under a canopy called a huppah. The huppah represents the new home they will set up and is an essential part of a Jewish wedding. Actually the couple do not have to marry in a synagogue at all; the canopy could be set up in the garden if they wished and it would still be a Jewish marriage, provided two people witness it. In Britain the weather can be unpredictable so most Jewish weddings are held in the synagogue. As part of the ceremony the bride and groom share a glass of wine, a symbol of celebration. After the wedding the reception may be held in the synagogue hall or at a nearby hotel.

At the end of life

When a person dies, the synagogue community helps the family to arrange the funeral and gives them all the support they need. The funeral does not take place in the synagogue; it is held at the hall at the cemetery. The rabbi and members of the synagogue congregation attend the funeral and burial.

Jewish weddings must take place under the huppah. The synagogue usually erects a huppah in front of the ark.

- **Do you like the idea of marking the stages of your life as a public affair or would you rather it was a private matter?**

- **In pairs decide at what age you think it is most realistic for young people to take on responsibility for their own religious life? Would it be the same for a girl as a boy?**

Design a poster to show the part a synagogue can play in the stages of someone's life.

Social events at the synagogue

Some Jewish communities meet together regularly for social activities.

This is a small part of the site at Bet She'an which dates back to 5000 BCE. There is a talk about this excavation at the synagogue opposite.

ACTIVITY A

- The Goldsack family are thinking of moving into the area. The family consists of parents David and Eve, Sarah aged 13, Dan aged 11 and Mandy who is 4. The family want to know whether Crawshaw Road Synagogue has much of a social life. Write back to Mrs Goldsack and tell her what sort of things might be on offer for the members of her family and for her elderly mother who often comes to stay.

- Look at the activities at the synagogue and sort them into three columns headed Educational, Social, and Worship.

- Find out:

  Who was Akiva?

  What is challah?

  What is the 'candle lighting' that is mentioned every Friday?

- Make up ten questions on any aspect of Judaism for use at the Intersynagogue Quiz on the 11th. You will need to supply the question-master with the answers on a separate sheet.

- Choose one of the events mentioned and write a report for the *Crawshaw Road Chronicle*, which is a monthly newletter produced by the synagogue.

- If you are interested in archaeology, you might like to try and find out about *Recent archaeology in Galilee*, which is the talk on the 26th. It investigates the current excavations at Bet She'an, a site just below Lake Galilee in Israel. An internet search would be a good way to start. One site which is useful is www.israel-mfa.gov.il.

CRAWSHAW ROAD SYNAGOGUE

This month's events

1 Thursday 2.30 p.m. Friendship Club for retired people: tea and speaker

2 Friday 6.30 p.m. Supper followed by candle lighting & Shabbat evening service

3 SHABBAT 11 a.m. service led by Rabbi Stephen Hill

4 Sunday 10 a.m. religion school for 5–12 yrs

7.30 p.m. music group

5 Monday 6.30–8.30 p.m.Girls' Group (11–14)

6 Tuesday 10 a.m.–4 p.m. Day Centre (lunch incl)

7.30 p.m. Crawshaw Road Debating Society

7 Wednesday 8 p.m. Council meeting for those elected to run the synagogue

7.30–9.30 p.m. Shalom Venture Scouts (15–21s) Rock Climbing

8 Thursday 2.30 p.m. Friendship Club for retired people, tea and bingo

9 Friday Candle lighting & Shabbat evening service

10 SHABBAT 11 a.m. Morning service

11 Sunday 10 a.m. Religion school

7 p.m. Intersynagogue Quiz (7 p.m. for 7.30 p.m.)

12 Monday 6.30–8.30 p.m. Girls' Group (11–14)

13 Tuesday 10 a.m.–4 p.m. Day Centre (lunch incl)

7 p.m. GCSE Hebrew for Year 10

14 Wednesday 8 p.m. Ladies Guild speaker on 'Baking Better Challah'

15 Thursday 2.30 p.m. Friendship Club for retired people: tea and entertainment

8 p.m. piano recital in Banqueting Hall

16 Friday Candle lighting & Shabbat service

17 SHABBAT 11 a.m. service

1 p.m. 'Learn Jewish Songs Workshop' after service

18 Sunday 10 a.m. Religion school

Sponsored walk in aid of homeless leaves synagogue at 1 p.m.

7.30 p.m. Music group

19 Monday 8 p.m. Bnei Akiva youth study group

6.30–8.30 p.m. Girls' Group ice-skating

20 Tuesday 10 a.m.–4 p.m. Day Centre (lunch included)

7 p.m. auditions for summer play.

21 Wednesday 7.30 p.m. Israeli Evening with traditional dancing

22 Thursday 2.30 p.m. Friendship Club for retired people: visit and tea

23 Friday 6.30 p.m. supper followed by candle lighting & Shabbat Evening Service

24 SHABBAT 11 a.m. morning service with Rabbi Stephen Hill

1 p.m. Torah study session

25 Sunday 10 a.m. Religion School

1 p.m. Family Fun Barbecue in school grounds

26 Monday 6.30–8.30 p.m. Girls' Group

'Recent Archaeology in Galilee' talk 7.45 p.m.

27 Tuesday 10 a.m.–4 p.m. Day Centre (lunch incl)

7 p.m. GCSE Hebrew for Year 10s

28 Wednesday 7.45 p.m. Jerusalem Saxophone Ensemble concert: tickets from Synagogue Office

29 Thursday 12.30 Friendship Club lunch for retired people

30 Friday Candle lighting & Shabbat service

To check on events above (or to buy tickets for special events) contact the Synagogue Office in person or ring.

Shalom Playgroup will continue to meet every weekday morning from 10 a.m–12 noon in the upstairs room.

Festivals

Everybody in a Jewish family does their best to return home for the Passover meal no matter where their job normally takes them. On the table is a special Seder plate that holds symbolic foods to remind the people present of the ancient story. Can you discover the meaning of the roasted egg; shank bone; lettuce; salt water; bitter herbs, wine, unleavened bread; and the sweet paste called Haroset?

Let us celebrate

We all like a reason to celebrate. It might be that someone in the family has passed an exam, has a birthday or gets engaged. Some of these events may be once in a lifetime, others more frequent, but often they only involve a small number of people. It is also fun to celebrate on a bigger scale, maybe with the whole school or the community. Festivals are a good reason for everybody to get together and enjoy themselves, send cards, give presents and eat good food. Festivals also happen every year so there is only a short wait for the next party.

Most festivals actually celebrate an event. Often it is a significant event in the community's past. Such a celebration commemorates the event and teaches the story to the new generation. The event may make people reflect on their own behaviour or their lifestyle.

Pesach

Pesach, or Passover, is the most important celebration in the Jewish calendar. It is based on the story of the Jews' rescue from slavery. Many people are familiar with the story of how Moses, following God's instructions, got the Jews out of Egypt after the ten plagues. You can read the full story in Exodus 12.

When Jewish people celebrate this festival today, they enjoy good food, wine and company but at the same time remember the serious message behind the celebrations. Jews are reminded that those who put their trust in God, and obey his commands, are not let down.

As a class, debate the following: *Celebrating the same thing every year gets boring.*

You will need one person to speak in favour of this motion and give reasons. You will also need another person to argue against the motion and give reasons. The debate should then be open to the floor, where other people in the class have the chance to add their views before you vote on it.

Write an essay to explain why most communities celebrate festivals. You could include specific examples of festivals that you enjoy celebrating. Be sure to mention the following points:

- The advantages gained from celebrating a regular festival.

- What people would miss out on if there were no festivals in the year.

- Give your own opinions at the end.

Write a report for the evening paper to go with the photograph. There is space for only 250 words.

ACTIVITY A Make a leaflet about Pesach from a sheet of folded A4 paper. Start by using the information given here then add your own research.

Or

Make a leaflet about Rosh Hashanah which appears on pages 88–89. If you prefer a completely new topic, research Hanukkah.

- Each leaflet needs to explain how Jews celebrate the festival at home and in the synagogue. Draw and label any symbolic foods. Make sure you explain the serious message behind the festival.

- Useful websites for research are

  www.re-xs.ucsm.ac.uk

  www.theresite.org.uk

  www.bbc.co.uk/worldservice/religion

  www.jewish.co.uk

In pairs, list six different family events that might be cause for celebration. Now think of six things a wider community – like the village, the town or the whole country – might want to celebrate. How will the celebrations differ?

New year – new start

January 1st

- *I won't eat so much junk food.*

- *I will try to get my homework done on time.*

- *I will write in my diary every ...*

It is always good to be given the chance to make a fresh start, to put the past behind you and begin again. This might be when you move up into the next year group at school, start a new job, or move house. Traditionally the start of a new calendar year is an opportunity for new year's resolutions. All too often, though, they are forgotten by the third day of January.

Celebration

On the first evening of Rosh Hashanah, the Jewish New Year, a family attends synagogue then returns home to enjoy a special meal together. For them it is not only a celebration of the start of the religious calendar, but an opportunity to celebrate the anniversary of the beginning of the world, in other words, Creation. Traditional foods like apples and honey are served to wish each other a full rounded year and the hope for a sweet new year.

Reflection

The beginning of the year is also a serious time. The future is always unknown but we hope things will work out well. Sometimes there are things you can do to set events off correctly; at other times you have to trust all will be well. What happens in the future is often affected by what happened in the past. Because of this, Jews spend ten days at new year reflecting on events in the past year. During these ten days arguments should be settled and apologies given for anything hurtful that was said or done. It is equally important for apologies to be accepted so that no grudges remain.

I really am sorry

The tenth day of Rosh Hashanah is the holiest day of the whole year. It is called Yom Kippur and is when Jews make their confession directly to God for all the sins they have committed during the previous year. To show they really are sorry and want God's forgiveness, Jews give up all personal pleasures for 25 hours. They fast, restrict themselves to only basic washing of hands, and do not wear perfume nor jewellery. All Jews, even those who rarely go to synagogue, try to attend one of the five synagogue services that day to make their confession.

The shofar is blown in the synagogue during the ten days of Rosh Hashanah and last heard on the day of Yom Kippur. The shofar is made of a ram's horn that is heated, twisted, polished and hollowed out. The sound of the shofar is strident and calls Jews to repentance. Hearing the shofar reminds Jews of the Day of Judgement when they will be answerable to God for their behaviour.

There is no point in dwelling on the past. That is over and done with. Do you think this is a sensible attitude to take? Can you see any problems with looking back over what you said and did? What advantages could there be?

● 'Forgive and forget'. What do people mean when they say that? Write a story where this actually happens.

● Find out why people, like the person in the picture, wear white at Yom Kippur?

Why do you think the ten days of Rosh Hashanah are also called the days of repentance?

ACTIVITY A

● Draw the two traditional foods eaten at Jewish New Year and write against each one what it symbolises.

● Research Janus, the Roman god who gives his name to the month of January. Find out how he was shown in statues. Make a sketch of his head. What is the similarity between the idea shown in that Roman statue and the Jewish attitude to new year? Do you think it is a helpful idea?

1 Name three different activities that might take place in a synagogue.
2 Write a leaflet that could be handed to non-Jewish visitors to an Orthodox synagogue. Explain the main features. Tell them what sort of activities take place at the synagogue. Do not forget to include advice to help women as well as men who might wish to attend a service.
3 In groups of three or four make a poster about *Jewish Worship*. It would need to cover public worship and private worship. It would be wise to research further about morning prayer at home. Try to use some quotations from prayers on your poster.
4 Write one sentence for each of the following words to make their meaning clear:

Mitzvot **Torah** **omnipotent**

synagogue **mezuzah** **ner tamid**

GOING FORWARD

1 Design a T-shirt Jewish children could wear for the Sunday school activities at the synagogue. It might be a good idea to include some Jewish symbols on it.
2 New year does not always start on 1 January. Find out when Muslims and Sikhs celebrate their new year and what each celebrates. The Inland Revenue, who collect income tax in Britain, have a different date for their new year. When is it?
3 Find out what the silver ornaments on the top of the scrolls are called. Find out what the lions symbolise.
4 Design a stained-glass window for a new synagogue. The theme is 'The Torah'.

Unit 4 ▶ WHAT DOES IT MEAN TO BE A SIKH?

Discovering the Sikhs

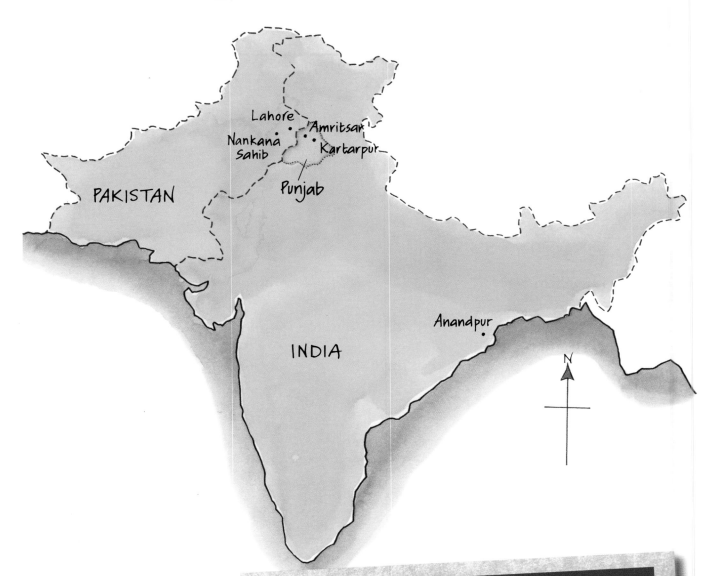

Fact box

- There are over 20 million Sikhs in the world.
- 80% live in north-west India in the area known as the Punjab.
- Half a million Sikhs live in Britain.
- Sikhism is the third largest religion in Britain.
- Sikhism is the youngest of the six world religions.
- 225 000 Sikhs live in Canada.
- 100 000 Sikhs live in the USA.

This is a very religious Sikh who has taken amrit. This means that he has decided to follow the rules of a particular lifestyle. As a sign of this a Sikh wears five symbolic objects. Because the name for each object begins with the letter K in Punjabi, they are known as the 5 Ks. Not all Sikhs wear all of the 5 Ks.

Kara – a steel bracelet that symbolises the oneness of God. More details about this are on page 94.

Kachera – white shorts worn as underclothes by men and women symbolise modesty.

Kangha – a comb tucked in the hair symbolising that Sikhs' lives should be disciplined and orderly.

Kirpan – this short dagger is worn in its sheath as a reminder that Sikhs have a duty to fight for the oppressed. The kirpan is usually worn by men and women under their clothing. To comply with the British law which forbids people to carry an offensive weapon in public, some Sikhs have a miniature kirpan on their kangha.

Kesh – no body hair is cut because hair is a gift from God. Sikhs must keep their hair clean and tidy. Women usually tie their hair back under a scarf and men wind their hair round like a knot on the top of the head and wear a turban.

ACTIVITY A

- To remind yourself of how Guru Nanak founded Sikhism listen to the story on www.bbc.co.uk/worldservice/people/sikhism

- If you have not studied the 5 Ks before, or need reminding about how they came into existence, look up information about the actions of the tenth Guru Gobind Singh at the festival of Vaisakhi in 1699 CE. The story is told briefly on page 124 or you can listen to it being read on www.bbc.co.uk/worldservice/people/sikhism_khal.shtm

- Find out more about the Punjab area. You could look on a CD-Rom or use an atlas.

  What is the population of the area?

  What other religions are in that area?

- Use the facts and figures that appear on this page to write an account of Sikhism in the world.

The Sikh view of God

This symbol is called Ik Onkar. It is made up of the figure one and the first letter of the Punjabi alphabet. This is the opening of the hymn called the Mool Mantra, which states Sikh beliefs about God. Many Sikhs have this symbol in their home and it helps them to keep God in mind.

The kara, or Sikh bracelet, was shown on page 93. Wearing it reminds Sikhs that God is one and has no beginning and no end. The bracelet is made of steel and not of a precious metal, to show that God is for everyone not just the well-off. The bracelet is worn loosely on the wrist so it drops forward as a Sikh works, reminding them to do good with their hands.

Life is a journey

Sikhs believe that everyone came from God in the beginning, so each person has God within him or her. This belief is central to Sikh teaching and means that people of all religions are equal. Sikhs say that they are Sikh because they were born into a Sikh family and they accept that other religions may also lead people to God by a different path.

The Sikh emphasis on equality means that everyone has the same direct access to God.

Sikhs spend their lives working along the path that leads towards God. Union with God is the most important goal for Sikhs. In order to achieve this they try to keep God in mind at all times, when worshipping and in daily life. In the following pages you will read of the different ways Sikhs try to maintain their focus on God.

Guru Nanak explained to his followers there is only one God. This belief is at the heart of Sikhism and summed up in the Mool Mantra. *Mool* means 'essence'. *Mantra* is a verse which is continually repeated. It sets out Sikh beliefs about God.

Mool Mantra

There is one God
Whose name is Truth
The creator
Without fear
Without hate
Immortal
Beyond birth and death,
Self-existent,
Made known by grace of the Guru

Sikhs accept that it is impossible for people to understand God, a power far superior to the human mind. Since God has no form it is impossible for us to imagine such a being. That also means that we can never definitively prove the existence of God.

Sikhs are sure that God is love and can never be found, only experienced in the human heart.

Copy the Mool Mantra into your exercise book setting it out as shown in the panel. Then use a different coloured pen to write a brief explanation alongside each line.

- Why would a Sikh think it was wrong to be rude about Christian beliefs?

- With a partner, work out a list of things that no one could prove, things that have to be taken on trust. Here's a start:

  next week will have a Saturday in it

  you will leave school at the end of Year 11.

Re-read the information given about the Sikh idea of God and compare it with the idea of God in another religion you have studied. In what ways do they differ?

Do you think that the religion a person follows might be just an accident of birth and geography? Could some people hold another view? What reasons would they give?

Meditating on God – nam simran

Throughout their lives Sikhs work towards union with God. The best way of doing this, they find, is to focus their mind on words for God. They choose one of their favourite names for God and quietly repeat it over and over again. The gentle chanting pushes away other busy thoughts and frees their minds to focus on God. This form of Sikh meditation is called *nam simran* and means 'remembering the name of God'.

> Meditation of the Lord is the highest of the deeds, through which myriads obtain release, through which the thirst (of desires) is quenched, through which one becomes all knowing, through which the fear of death goes away, through which all the desires are fulfilled, through which the dirt of the mind is cleansed and the Nectar of the name of God is absorbed in the mind.
>
> Guru Nanak

> The highest of all religions is to meditate on God and live a pure life.
>
> Guru Arjan

The technique a Sikh uses to meditate:

1 Choose one of the names for God that inspires feelings of faith.
2 Begin to recite the name aloud.
3 Reduce the sound down to a whisper and start to hear the words in the mind.
4 Close the eyes and hear the words recited in the mind.

The purpose of nam simran

Sikhs believe that meditation gets rid of all anxieties and fears that tie them down. By freeing the mind of daily stresses, Sikhs not only feel better and happier, but they grow closer to God. Guru Granth Sahib says nam is the best remedy for all ills. It means if your mind is calm and peaceful, then you can deal with any challenges.

ਨਾਮੁ ਖੁਮਾਰੀ ਨਾਨਕਾ, ਚੜੀ ਰਹੇ ਦਿਨ ਰਾਤਿ ॥

(1469 - 1539) Shree Guru Nank Dev Ji

Guru Nanak stressed the importance of constantly keeping God in mind. This picture shows the guru in a traditional meditation pose but Sikhs do not have to sit in this pose. Sikhism teaches that you can think about God at any time, in any place. If Sikhs are working with their hands or feet, the guru said it was possible to turn their minds to God and quietly repeat the name. Working and meditating are considered the best form of worship.

> *wahe-guru* – are the most frequently used words for meditation; they mean 'wonderful teacher'.
>
> *Sat nam* – some Sikhs use this name for God when they meditate; it means 'true name'.
>
> *Akal purakh* – this name for God 'means the eternal, the timeless one'.

When do Sikhs meditate?

Nam simran can be done at any time. Some Sikhs use meditation as part of their own morning worship. After getting up and washing, they sit quietly and meditate before they recite the morning prayer. Guru Arjan thought it was a good way to start the day because, he said, *Meditating on the Lord cleans the scum of your mind.* Nam simran plays an important part in congregational worship and some Sikhs find great spiritual strength in chanting the words with others.

One Sikh teacher said the ideal way of living is like the child flying a kite in the sky. He can chat happily with his friends, but he never loses sight of the kite. In the same way, the teacher said, people are happiest in life if they always keep God in mind.

- What does a Sikh mean by meditation?
- How is this different from saying prayers?
- Some Sikhs say they can manage nam simran far better with their busy lifestyles than set prayers. Why is that the case?

How easy do you find it to empty your mind? If somebody says think about nothing, can you do it? What do you find is the best technique for calming yourself down when you are upset about something?

How would a Sikh reply if someone said, 'Nam simran is just reciting words like a parrot'?

Outside the Guru's door

This is a purpose-built gurdwara of a Sikh sect in Birmingham. The strings of flags are flying to celebrate a festival but you can see the Nishan Sahib flying higher than the other flags. The dome copies the traditional shape of a gurdwara in the Punjab and symbolises the kingship, or authority, of the holy scriptures.

Like all religious groups, the Sikhs have their own special place of worship. This originally grew up around the first teacher, Guru Nanak. His followers settled near him in Kartarpur and usually met in the early mornings and at sunset to sing hymns he had composed. They often shared a meal together afterwards. Later, gurus developed a building with the holy scriptures inside and a langar (with dining room and kitchen). No special day was set aside as holy. Sikhs today tend to meet for worship at the gurdwara on a Sunday because that is the day most people are free from work.

The guru's door

The word gurdwara is made up of two parts, which translate as 'the guru's door'. The building gets this name because it is the way to the guru, the holy scriptures called the Guru Granth Sahib.

Gurdwara is sometimes translated as 'the house of God' even though Sikhs believe God is everywhere and not restricted to a building. Guru Granth Sahib says, 'The Holy Book is the abode of God'. So, wherever the scriptures are, there is God.

Congregation + scriptures = gurdwara

In addition to the Guru Granth Sahib, the building needs a congregation of people. Sikhs believe that one is not effective without the other. For Sikhs, the gurdwara is both a place of worship and the heart of their social life, and many events take place there. The presence of Guru Granth Sahib gives the building its authority.

All gurdwaras have a langar, which is a kitchen and dining room where meals are prepared and freely given to anyone who sits down there.

Nishan Sahib

A gurdwara is usually recognised by the saffron-coloured flag that flies outside the front. It is called Nishan Sahib which means 'guru's symbol' and shows that the building is a gurdwara housing the Guru Granth Sahib. The Sikh Khanda, or double edged sword, is in the middle and has a circle, called Chakar, with two swords either side. The pole has the same coloured material as the flag wrapped all the way up to the top. Once a year at the festival of Vasaikhi the congregation removes the old flag and material, washes the pole, then hoists a new flag (see page 124). This will fly at full-mast for the rest of the year.

This gurdwara is in Birmingham. Not all Sikh communities can afford to build a gurdwara exactly as they would like. Many communities have to convert a house or similar building. The Nishan Sahib shows that this is a gurdwara. The flag pole is also covered with the same material as the flag. The top of the pole is crowned by the Sikh Khanda or double-edged sword.

- How does the gurdwara get its name?
- What would you look for outside if you were unsure whether the building was a gurdwara?

With a partner discuss the advantages and disadvantages of having a place of worship clearly defined by symbols.

ACTIVITY A Fold an A4 sheet of paper in half. On the cover write 'Welcome to the Gurdwara'. Inside, begin to give a visitor some idea of what a gurdwara is. You will be able to add other double pages to the leaflet with details of the inside of the building.

Prayer hall

The musicians.

Men sit on the floor here.

Canopy over Guru Granth Sahib.

ਤੇਰੀ ਓ ੮ ਸੀ ਗੁਰੂ ਤੇਗ ਬਹਾਦਰ ਗੁਰਦਵਾਰਾ

The manji sahib is the stool that holds the Guru Granth Sahib.

Picture of Guru Nanak.

Women sit on the floor here.

The takht is the platform that holds the holy book.

Offerings are put in front of Guru Granth Sahib. This might be food, flowers or money.

Features in the prayer hall

The picture on page 100 shows only one of several rooms in the gurdwara. It is the prayer hall and, because it houses the Guru Granth Sahib, is the most important room in any gurdwara. Some large gurdwaras may have several prayer halls. For instance, the large gurdwara shown on page 91 has four large prayer halls and a further small one inside the highest dome on the roof. Here the first hymns of the day are sung between 5 a.m. and 7 a.m. At weekends all the large prayer halls can be busy with weddings with over a thousand guests visiting the gurdwara.

Important features in the prayer hall

The takht is the platform in the centre of the prayer hall and holds the Guru Granth Sahib. It is raised, showing the importance of the scriptures to Sikhs. The canopy over the book shows respect for the book in the same way that someone in India might hold a sunshade over the head of an important person to protect him.

Donations are placed near Guru Granth Sahib. Money is dropped into the box in front of the takht as the worshippers approach and bow to the book. Donations may also take the form of food which is first offered in the prayer hall and then taken to the langar to be cooked and used.

Pictures of Guru Nanak are often found on the walls in the gurdwara. Sometimes other gurus are shown as well, along with pictures of the Golden Temple at Amritsar. Sikhs do not worship the pictures nor do they worship the gurus. The pictures are there to help them focus their mind on God.

Seating in the gurdwara is on the floor. Guru Nanak sat on the ground with his followers to show that everyone was equal. Men and women usually sit on opposite sides in a gurdwara because it is traditional to sit separately in India. Both are equal; neither group sits closer to the Guru Granth Sahib than the other.

Compare the prayer hall in this picture with the one on page 100-101.

ACTIVITY A

Add a further folded A4 sheet to your 'Welcome to the gurdwara' leaflet.

- Give details of what a visitor might see in the prayer hall.

- Explain what the features are.

- Tell visitors how they should behave in the gurdwara, including which appropriate clothing to wear. You will find more information on this in the next few pages as well.

- Continue adding other material to your booklet as you work through the next few pages.

The heart of the community

The langar

The langar is the most obvious sign that the gurdwara does put its beliefs into practice. The food which was seen offered in front of the holy book on page 100 was given freely. This, along with all the other food that has been given, is prepared and served by volunteers. It is served to any person who walks into the langar. Food served in the langar is always vegetarian because Sikhs believe that everyone will then be able to eat it. (At home many Sikhs do eat meat.) Worshippers in the prayer hall usually stay to share a meal with others. The gurdwara willingly feeds homeless people, even those who have no particular religion and may have been sleeping rough. They are served with the same food and respect as everyone else. The only rule that applies to anyone entering the gurdwaras is that they must not be drunk, nor carry alcohol, drugs or tobacco. Guru Nanak taught that these items make people senseless, which often leads to wickedness.

The shoe room

Because Sikhs remove their shoes before entering the prayer hall, a special area is set aside for their shoes to be kept. Often a fellow-Sikh chooses to

look after the shoes and dusts them for other worshippers. This service is dealt with in more detail on page 118. Near the shoe racks is a washbasin so that worshippers can wash their hands and cover their heads, as part of their preparation before going into the prayer hall.

The library

All gurdwaras have some books that are helpful to the Sikh community. In a small gurdwara the library may only amount to a couple of shelves, but in a large gurdwara a whole room may be set aside. In addition to books to help with worship, there are books about learning the Punjabi language as well as plenty of books written in the language. There might also be books about the Punjabi homeland and its traditions, with cookery and music being particular favourites.

ACTIVITY A
Draw up your own ground floor plan for a gurdwara. Remember that the prayer hall is the most important room but try and include some of the features mentioned above.

Rest rooms

All gurdwaras offer accommodation for travellers. The very large gurdwara on page 91 can accommodate up to five hundred overnight visitors but this is unusual. Most can host a small number of visitors, perhaps Sikhs who are travelling from one gurdwara to another, someone who has become homeless, or a holy person arriving for a special festival.

Other parts of the gurdwara

A large gurdwara may have several rooms used as offices by members of the community elected to run the gurdwara. Some rooms are used for education, like language classes in English or Punjabi. Many Sikhs are keen to learn music and singing which have an important place in worship. Sikh youth groups or women's groups may hold meetings in the gurdwara.

Large gurdwaras can have other facilities. In India some have a medical centre attached and carry out free eye operations on whoever requires them. In Africa, one gurdwara has a college attached to it and accepts anyone who wants to study there. The large Birmingham gurdwara on page 91 has a factory complex attached to it, which provides paid employment for anyone who requires it. This puts into practice the Sikh belief that everybody who is fit should earn an honest living. Sikhs do not believe in begging or living off other people.

- Why would you be unlikely to find a Sikh begging on the streets?

- Guru Amar Das said: 'Each gives as much as he can spare and takes as much as he needs. Here there is no difference between kings and beggars. All can sit together and eat simple food served with loving care.' Explain exactly what the guru was talking about.

- What functions would you say the gurdwara performs in the community?

What is the Guru Granth Sahib?

The Sikh holy scriptures are known as the Guru Granth Sahib. As you will remember, guru means teacher and these particular writings are the present-day teacher for Sikhs. Ten human gurus taught people for over two hundred years, but Guru Gobind Singh told his followers he would be the last. Instead, people would have a spiritual guide in the form of a book. The word Granth means 'a large book'. The holy writings were called Guru Granth to show that this was the teacher. Sahib is a term of respect, like calling a male teacher 'sir'.

Collecting the writings

The writings in Guru Granth Sahib were collected together over a long period of time. The second guru, Guru Angad received the writings of Guru Nanak. The fifth guru wrote down Guru Nanak's hymns that were inspired by God. Hymns and poetry of later gurus, also believed to have been inspired by God, went into the collection. It was finished in 1604 CE.

This poster on the wall of a gurdwara shows the Guru Granth Sahib in the centre.

The Sikh scriptures are unusual because they contain writings by people from other religions. Of the 5894 verses in the book, 938 were written by Muslim and Hindu holy men. Sikhs believe that God is revealed to people of all races and religions and they are prepared to listen to the truth wherever it comes from.

Every copy is 1430 pages long and the words appear in exactly the same place on a page in all copies of the book.

Extracts from the Guru Granth Sahib

Love is the password that takes us to the door of God.

When a lamp is lit darkness is dispelled. Similarly by reading religious books, the darkness of the mind is destroyed.

When a herdsman comes to grazing land does he come to stay? Why are you so vain as to think you can stay for ever? When the time of your life is over you will have to move on. So set your affairs in order. Think of your real home. Sing God's praises and serve the Guru with love. What is there to be proud of? Like an overnight guest you must leave at dawn. Why be too attached to home and family? They are short-lived like flowers in a garden. Think of God, who provided everything you have. Leave everything else behind.

All other forms of life are subject to you (humans), your rule is on this earth.

Sikh scriptures include writings from other religions. What do you think that says about the Sikh attitude to other religions?

The importance of Guru Granth Sahib

As the Sikhs' spiritual guide, the holy scriptures are at the heart of all Sikh worship. They are used at ceremonies marking important stages of a person's life (see pages 122–123).

Advice is sometimes sought by 'taking a vak'. That means the book is opened at random and the first passage read from the left-hand page. Sikhs believe this method enables God's advice to be given to people.

On special occasions there can be a continuous reading of the scriptures which lasts 48 hours. It is called the Akhand path and may mark a significant event in life, like a marriage, death or a special festival. Every two hours a new reader takes over (see pages 110–111).

- Read the extracts from Guru Granth Sahib. Explain in your own words what the longest passage is about.

- Look at the poster showing the ten gurus with the holy scriptures. In your exercise book list as many religious features as you can identify in the poster. Here are some prompts:

  What is the name of the first guru who appears top left?

  The final human guru appears third from the left on the bottom line. Who is he?

  What is the name of the writing on the poster?

  What is the symbol that appears above the holy book and what does it mean?

  Explain what the Khanda is and what each part means.

The importance of the Guru Granth Sahib

The holy book is enthroned on the manji sahib to show the kingship of the word of God. Beautiful cloths, called romalas, are used to wrap the book when it is not in use.

The heart of the gurdwara

The picture of the inside of the prayer hall on page 100 gave a clear idea of how important Guru Granth Sahib is. All worshippers face it and sit at a lower level, in the same way as they would sit at the feet of a great teacher in India. All the people who enter the prayer hall at the gurdwara have taken off their shoes, covered their heads with a scarf or turban and washed their hands. Worshippers walk in and go straight to the takht and bow down, touching their forehead on the carpet. This is not worshipping a book, it is showing respect for the words of God. Offerings are made to God at this time. Coins are often placed in the donations box at the front on the floor, and gifts of food or flowers are laid alongside. Worshippers avoid turning their back on Guru Granth Sahib as they return to sit down and they do not sit with their feet facing the book. This is considered rude in Indian society.

VIP

Many little gestures of respect are paid to the words of God in the same way respect would be paid to a very important person. As a living guru, the book represents a VIP. Not only is it placed on a throne, or takht, but a canopy symbolically protects it from the sun. The book is never left unattended in the prayer hall. A Sikh sits behind the book and periodically waves a chauri over it, symbolically keeping it free of flies and dust in the same way as they would care for an important person.

The scriptures rest comfortably on cushions on the manji and are wrapped in precious materials called romalas. These are given by Sikhs as a token of respect for the word of God and also to keep the book clean.

The Guru Granth Sahib is not only at the heart of the gurdwara, it is at the heart of a Sikh's life. Its contents guide Sikh beliefs and behaviour.

This is a very ornate bedroom. You can see the four-poster bed with lace drapes and, under the duvet, two wrapped books are visible. In all gurdwaras the copies of the Guru Granth Sahib are wrapped in beautiful material and rest in a bed (with other copies) when not in use. A human guru would be shown similar respect. At the beginning of the day, the book that is to be used is carried from the bedroom, still wrapped in its cloth, on someone's head. Everyone stands to face the book as it passes.

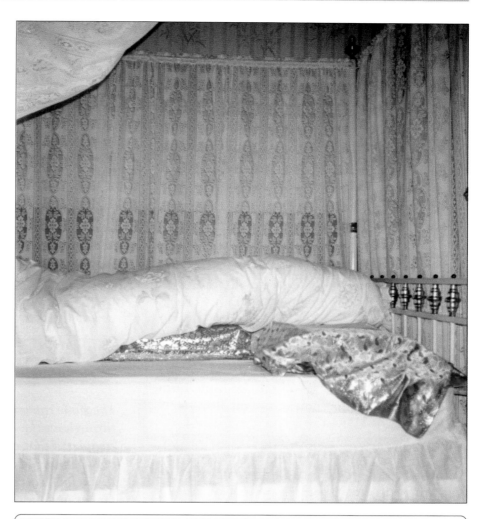

- With a partner compile a list of the special things a town might do for an official visit from the queen. Work out why they are going to so much bother and expense. Who do you think gets the most out of the event? The queen undertakes lots of visits like this every year; the townspeople may only get such a visit once in their lifetime.

- Many of the customary ways of showing respect to Guru Granth Sahib come from the Punjab homeland. What different ways could someone show respect to a very important book or person if the customs had originated in the West?

- Think about the pros and cons of replacing a classroom teacher with a book. Draw two columns in your exercise book. Head one, Advantages and the other, Disadvantages. Fill in your ideas in each column. At the end write a few sentences giving your conclusion about which you would prefer.

- How important is the Guru Granth Sahib? Give some examples of how the holy book is treated to support your answer.

- On a double page in your book draw and label a spider diagram to show the ways Guru Granth Sahib is respected as a living guru.

The Akhand path

This is what Guru Arjan said about the value of the holy scriptures:

> In the platter are placed three things, truth, contentment, and meditation. The nectar, the name of God, the support of all has also been put in it. Whoever eats this food, whoever relishes it, becomes spiritually liberated.

Guru Arjan also said:

> Meditate fearlessly on the Supreme One. In the company of the devout encourage others also to meditate.

Guru Amar Das said:

> Anyone can see the Guru. Mere sight does not bring spiritual liberation. This comes from meditating on the holy word.

Also from the Guru Granth Sahib comes the following extract:

> The most virtuous act is that of talking about God. By listening to God's word sorrows and sufferings disappear.

Where will the Akhand path be?

Sikhs can arrange a continuous reading of the Guru Granth Sahib to take place at their home, their business or in the gurdwara. Most will choose the gurdwara because it requires a great deal of preparation and space to have the holy book brought to your home or workplace. One room must be specially cleaned and set aside exclusively for Guru Granth Sahib, who will be an honoured guest. For the duration of the Guru's stay, that room becomes a gurdwara and everyone who enters the room must behave accordingly.

 LOOKING BACK

Look back to page 108 to remind yourself of how people must behave.

The same copy of the Guru Granth Sahib is used throughout the Akhand path but when the reading is completed that copy is taken to rest. Another copy of the holy book will be brought out for use in the gurdwara. If you look carefully in this picture you can see the Ik Onkar and the Sikh symbol. The donation box is just visible on the floor in front of Guru Granth Sahib and the beautiful romala which covers the holy book can be seen to the right. This will be wrapped around the copy when the Akhand path is finished.

Why have an Akhand path?

Sikhs believe that they can receive God's blessings by listening to Guru Granth Sahib. An Akhand path will take place at festival time and is often requested at other significant times. This could be when a family is about to move house or begin a new business venture. It might also mark an important stage in the life of one member of the family, a birth, an impending marriage, or after a family death.

The reading usually takes place over three days, ending on the morning of the third day. During this time friends and family members call in at various times. Other members of the congregation are welcome and many choose to attend. Karah parshad is given to everyone and the langar serves food throughout the 48 hours. If the Akhand path takes place in a house, food will also be given to everyone who calls in. Even during the night people can be found quietly sitting, listening and meditating on the words of the scripture.

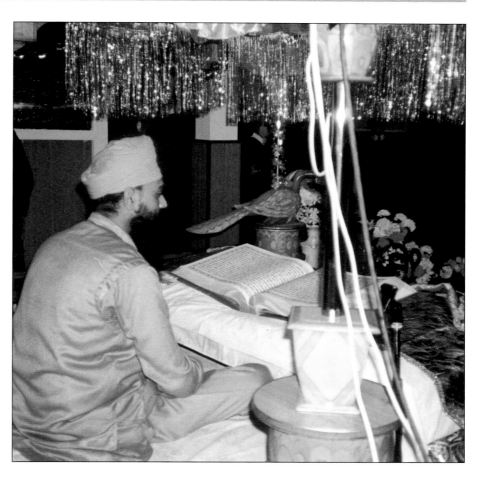

No person reads for more than two hours at a time in case he or she gets tired and makes mistakes. Another reader is always ready to take over if the first reader feels unwell and needs to leave.

Sadharan path

This is similar to the Akhand path in that the whole of Guru Granth Sahib is read, but it differs because the reading is not continuous. A Sadharan path often takes place when a family is in mourning. Sections of Guru Granth Sahib are read over nine days at convenient times for the family.

> **Look at the words of Guru Arjan. What does he suggest a Sikh might gain from listening to Guru Granth Sahib?**

> **Why do you think a family in mourning might prefer a Sadharan path to an Akhand path?**
>
> **What do you think a Sikh starting a new job might gain from an Akhand path?**
>
> **With a partner consider:**
>
> - **How could Sikhs receive God's blessings through an Akhand path?**
>
> - **Why is the distribution of Karah parshad part of an Akhand path?**
>
> - **Can you think of any occasion when you chanced to hear a song, a piece of poetry or something somebody said, that really made you think?**

Prayer

Why do Sikhs pray?

Sikhs believe that prayer is a natural response to God, who gives grace without any reference to our merit.

- By praying, Sikhs believe they are opening themselves to God's presence and power. Their aim is to draw closer to God and they believe prayer can help them do this.

- Being thankful. If you reflect back on today, there have probably been several instances when you have been grateful for something that someone has said or done for you. You may have told the person. Thanking God for his grace to us, which might be in the form of food supplied, friendship, happiness or any gift, is perfectly natural.

- Seeking help. It is likely that you have asked a teacher for help recently. That is not unusual. Maybe the last time you asked a teacher for help, you probably wanted help to do something yourself. You did not ask the teacher to do it for you. Sikhs see it as normal to ask God's assistance in something they are going to do; they would not expect God to do it for them. Some Sikhs ask for God's blessing. It might be for a journey they are undertaking, or a new job they are starting. They do not think God will change his actions as a result, but they hope to gain the courage or strength to deal with the challenge themselves.

Sikhs, like most religious communities, find great spiritual strength in worshipping in a group.

- Praying for those who need help. This might seem a waste of time, if Sikhs do not expect God to change his plans. What they say is, if you pray for others, it will put them in your mind and if you genuinely care about them, it will make you do something to help those people.

These are two extracts from the Japji, the most important Sikh prayer that was written by Guru Nanak. Some Sikhs start the day by reciting the whole of this prayer.

> God knows our needs and gives accordingly.
> Japji

> By God's will is everything created.
> His will cannot, however, be defined.
> By God's will there is life.
> By his will, we are honoured.
> By his will, we are placed high and low.
> It is by God's orders that we receive pleasure and pain.
> If he wills, he will be kind,
> Otherwise we move in transmigration forever.
> In short, all are subject to God's will,
> Nothing is outside it.
> Nanak says, 'If you realise the importance of God's will you will cease to be egotistic.
> Japji

Any way, anywhere, any time

Sikh prayer can be very informal. Sikhs believe that what matters most is the intention behind the prayer. A couple of lines from the Guru Granth Sahib recited while washing the dishes could be far more meaningful than any amount of set prayers in the gurdwara, so long as the person concentrates wholeheartedly on what is said.

While prayer is important in worship, Sikhs believe that it is not enough. True worship involves three important actions:

- doing good deeds to others - sewa
- leading a truthful life
- keeping God in mind.

Guru Nanak said that the company you keep can influence the way you behave. Think back to a few situations you have been in where you were affected by everybody else's attitude. Was it always bad?

- Write a story describing a situation where somebody was influenced towards good, against their will!

Look at the quotations from the Japji prayer. List three things it says God is responsible for in our lives.

Sikhs say you should do your best and leave the results to God. Why is that?

Music in worship

The musicians who play in the gurdwara are called ragis. Men or women, young or old, can learn to become a ragi. The musicians sit near Guru Granth Sahib in the gurdwara. Most of their hymns come from the holy book.

Unusual instruments

The musicians, or ragis, play instruments which are not familiar in the west. The drums are called tabla and two are usually used. The treble drum is narrower at the top and made of wood. A goat skin is stretched over it and attached by leather straps. Rolls of wood are tucked down the side and are pushed up or down to tighten or loosen the straps. This tunes the drum. The treble drum is played with fingertips, middle joints and the flat of the hand.

The bass drum is wider at the top and its body is usually made of metal. Fingertips, the whole palm and the heel of the hand are used to play this.

The harmonium is played with one hand while the other is used to pump the bellows.

The ragis also sing as they play. This religious singing is called kirtan and is sung slowly and steadily so everyone can hear and understand the words.

You can hear ragis performing music online at www.Sikhs.org or www.Sikhnet.com

In the mood

Music can put us in a certain mood. Listen to music in the background of television adverts or during a film. There is a clear difference between the music for a car chase, a haunted scene or a romantic encounter.

Guru Nanak realised how helpful music could be in calming people. He also noticed that people found it far easier to remember the words of songs than of poetry or prose. This led him to compose verses which could be sung to popular tunes of the day. One of his close friends, a Muslim musician, played a stringed instrument called a rabab which is similar to a guitar. This led to hymns becoming an important part of Sikh worship.

Food for the soul

Sikhs say the ragis' music is 'food for the soul' because it enables them to get closer to God. Most of the hymns are from the Guru Granth Sahib and called shabads. Singing them helps worshippers to think about the words of their great teachers.

For Sikhs, music is more than just a pleasant background sound in the gurdwara. It is a religious experience in itself, helping worshippers to become more God-centred.

- **Write an article for a music magazine to explain how music is used to help Sikhs worship in the gurdwara.**

- **With a partner discuss what pieces of music you would choose to:**

  put you in a cheerful frame of mind

  calm you down when you are stressed

  inspire you to get up and go.

- **Where do the musicians sit in the gurdwara and why?**

- **Write one sentence for each of these words to show you understand their meaning: ragi, kirtan, shabad, tabla.**

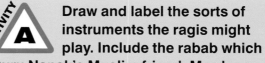

ACTIVITY A Draw and label the sorts of instruments the ragis might play. Include the rabab which Guru Nanak's Muslim friend, Mardana, played. Some ragis play that today.

Karah parshad

Karah parshad is simple to make.

You need an equal weight of:

plain wheat flour or semolina

sugar

ghee (clarified butter)

or ordinary butter

Melt the butter and gently mix in the flour. Cook for five minutes.

A quantity of water equal to the combined weight of the other ingredients is brought to the boil. Dissolve the sugar in it. Stir this liquid into the flour mixture.

Sikhs show their belief that God's blessings are given to everyone by offering each person in the prayer hall a small amount of karah parshad, or holy food. The mixture is prepared in an iron bowl and the words of the Japji prayer are recited as it is prepared. When the bowl of karah parshad is brought into the prayer hall a hymn of thanksgiving is recited and prayers offered as a kirpan is used to stir it. The Guru Granth Sahib is opened at random and the first passage from the left-hand page is read to the congregation.

Anyone can distribute karah parshad. It is usually given at the end of a service but if the worship goes on a long time, someone will walk around and hand some to newcomers in the room.

At the end of worship someone will carry the bowl and put a small ball of the mixture into each person's hand. The receivers remain seated and the person giving out the karah parshad, who can be male or female, puts it into their cupped hands.

The distribution of karah parshad is a very significant act. Everyone who is present is offered it. By sharing food from the same bowl all are reminded of the equality and the unity of humanity.

Karah parshad is only given out when worship has taken place in the presence of Guru Granth Sahib. That could be at a daily service or a ceremony to name a baby, a marriage or after a funeral. On special occasions the family often donate the ingredients for the karah parshad so God's blessings can be distributed.

- **List the religious stages of making karah parshad that turn it from just a mixture into holy food.**
- **Why is karah parshad given out?**
- **When and where might you receive karah parshad?**

Can you think of any other foods that are blessed and symbolically shared in the Christian religion?

ACTIVITY A Draw a bowl with a kirpan stirrer in the centre of a page in your exercise book. To the left of this write down how karah parshad becomes a holy food and to the right explain what it represents.

Some people say that karah parshad is a short version of the langar. What is the connection?

May I help you?

Because Sikhs believe that God is in everyone, helping a person is like helping God. Guru Nanak taught his followers that anything they did to help a person drew them closer to God. The word sewa is used to describe this service to others. The action has to be done without anybody asking you to do it and without any intention of being rewarded or noticed for doing it. One of Guru Nanak's successors warned: *'Whoever acts arrogantly while serving is not serving at all.'*

People visiting a gurdwara for the first time are often surprised to come across a person quietly brushing the front step, or when they get inside, see someone carefully going along the shoe racks, wiping the dust off the shoes that were placed there. This very humble activity is regarded as much a part of worship as listening to hymns in the prayer hall.

The gurdwara offers many opportunities for Sikhs to help others. Money and food can be donated for use in the gurdwara. Men and women of all ages assist in the preparation of the food, serving food to others, washing dishes and keeping the langar swept clean.

There are three forms of Sewa.

- **Tan** is doing something to help the community. It might be cleaning shoes at the gurdwara, washing up in the langar or helping to repair the building.
- **Man** is a mental service. It may involve studying the Guru Granth Sahib and teaching it to others.
- **Dhan** involves giving to people. Some Sikhs may give money or food to charity.

Since the beginning of Sikhism, Guru Nanak made it clear that everyone was created by God, so everyone was equal. That means that a Sikh should give sewa to everyone, no matter what religion or race they are. In the beginning not all Sikhs understood this. There is a story of a battle in which Guru Gobind Singh and his followers became involved when their town was attacked. After the battle some Sikhs were horrified to see Bhai Ghanaya, one of their own, giving water and first-aid to enemy soldiers. When the man was hauled before Guru Gobind Singh as a traitor, he explained that he saw no enemies on the battlefield, only his brothers. The Guru told his followers that Bhai Ghanaya had behaved as a true Sikh in treating everyone alike. *'It is our duty to help all people who are suffering and in need.'*

Nanak stressed the importance of sewa and put his own beliefs into action. When he settled down as a farmer, Nanak shared his earnings with those in need. Anyone who turned up at his door was welcome to share his family meals. This developed into the first langar.

As long as you breathe, keep doing service to others. This is how you will attain God.

Guru Nanak said:

A place in God's court can only be attained if we do service to others in this world.

Nothing is fruitful without service, for that is the essence of matter.

This man is one of many Sikhs in this community who give up some spare time to assist with the building of an extension to the front of the large gurdwara on page 91. This man is a professional bricklayer but he gets no money for working here. This is a part of sewa and he is happy to have the opportunity to give it. As he works, he quietly meditates on the name of God.

- What sort of sewa do you think a Sikh child could do at the gurdwara?

- Choose one of Guru Nanak's sayings and explain in your own words what he means. Can you think of a practical way a Sikh could follow those words?

- Why do Sikhs think it is important to serve other people?

- Which form of sewa is the man who is building the gurdwara extension performing?

ACTIVITY A On a double page in your exercise book write the word **SEWA** in the centre. Draw or cut out pictures to illustrate the different activities a Sikh could do to perform sewa.

Equality

Since the days of Guru Nanak, equality has been an important issue for Sikhs. Guru Nanak was born into an Indian society based on the caste system. This meant that people were born into a certain social group, or caste, because their parents belonged to that caste. Where those people lived, what rights they had, who they could mix with and even who they could marry, was determined by the caste they were born into. People had different parts to play in society. Those born into a high caste enjoyed comfortable lifestyles while those in the untouchables, at the bottom, had a grim existence. It was impossible for people to move out of their caste.

> **How much of a class system do you think exists in Britain today? Do some people receive better treatment than others in shops, jobs or education?**

Guru Nanak's encounter with God taught him that all human beings are the creation of God. Everyone is of equal worth in the eyes of God so it would be wrong to treat some people as inferior to others. This teaching has shaped Sikh attitudes towards women, racism and other religions.

The ninth guru gave his life for religious freedom. What is perhaps even more impressive, is that although he was a Sikh, he died in support of the Hindus' right to practise their religion. Guru Tegh Bahadur took the brave step of going to Emperor Aurangzeb, who forced everyone in his country to become a Muslim, to plead for religious tolerance. The guru was instantly thrown into prison, tortured and executed.

Guru Gobind Singh, the last human guru, also stressed that Sikhs must recognise the oneness of all humanity. *'Though they use different dresses according to the influence of regional customs, all men have the same eyes, ears, body and figure made out of the compounds of earth, air, fire and water.'*

> **Look through this unit on Sikhism and list at least five ways in which Sikhs put their belief in equality into practice. Things to look at are: karah parshad, seating in the gurdwara, the langar, etc.**

> **How far do you think equality between men and women is possible? Is equality between the sexes a good idea or could it be going against nature? Can you think of any situations where you would honestly prefer to be helped by somebody of the same sex?**
>
> **Find out more about the Hindu caste system. Look particularly at what Mahatma Gandhi did to break down prejudices.**

> **Sikhs believe in sexual equality.**
>
> - **How far do you think they have achieved this? Areas you might research further are the ten gurus, women's clothing and arranged marriages, and further education for girls.**
>
> - **Consider how a Sikh might respond to your points. Christians also believe in sexual equality. You might like to compare how far this religion has achieved sexual equality.**

Sikh policemen in Britain are permitted to wear a turban instead of the standard issue police helmet if they wish. What religious reason is there for this? Do you think exceptions should be made to rules on the grounds on religion? Can you think of any examples where other religions have different arrangements to accommodate their religious beliefs? Areas to think about might be diet, blood transfusions and clothing.

Life events at the gurdwara

Welcoming a baby

Sikhs believe a baby is a precious gift from God. About two weeks after the birth, the parents take their child to the gurdwara. During the service they give thanks for their baby and consult the Guru Granth Sahib about the child's name. The granthi takes a vak. He, or she, opens the scriptures at random and reads out the first hymn on the left-hand page. The first letter of the hymn is used for the baby's name. Sikhs believe this enables God to play a part in selecting a child's name. The family return at a later date to tell the community what name has been chosen.

After the family has been given the letter for their baby's name, they leave the gurdwara and select a suitable name. They may ask other members of the family or look through a book like this which gives the meaning of the names as well.

The true God has sent the child,

The long-lived child has been born by destiny.

When he came and acquired an abode in the womb

His mother's heart became very glad.

(This hymn was composed by Guru Arjan to celebrate the birth of his son.)

A Sikh wedding can only take place in the gurdwara because it must be in the presence of Guru Granth Sahib. The couple sit immediately in front of the holy book for the ceremony.

Marrying at the gurdwara

Sikhs believe that everyone should marry as part of their religious development. Through sharing their life with another person, it is believed they are brought closer to God. A marriage must take place in the presence of the Guru Granth Sahib and witnesses to be a Sikh marriage.

The ragis sing hymns from the holy book as the bride and groom come in. After explaining that Sikh marriage is a spiritual union, the granthi asks bride and groom if they are freely entering into the marriage. To show their acceptance, the couple bow to the holy book. The couple walk slowly around Guru Granth Sahib as the granthi recites the wedding hymn of Guru Ram Das.

The ceremony ends with the granthi taking a vak. The scriptures are opened and a passage read before karah parshad is given to all.

- When a husband and wife sit side by side why should we treat them as two? Outwardly separate, their bodies distinct, yet inwardly joined as one.
- They are not man and wife who only have physical contact, only they are wedded truly who have one spirit in two bodies.

Explain what the Sikh attitude towards a Register Office wedding would be.

A Sikh funeral

Some Sikhs request that the coffin be taken to the prayer hall of the gurdwara before the funeral but it is more usual for the coffin to go straight to the crematorium. As the coffin is carried in many Sikhs recite *Wahe-guru*. The granthi recites the Sohilla, the evening prayers and then, as the coffin slides into the furnace, the congregation recite the morning prayer.

Family mourning lasts for ten days and focuses on the words of Guru Granth Sahib. There may be a continuous reading, the Akhand path, at the gurdwara or sections are read over a number of days. This may be done at the gurdwara or at home.

- The dawn of a new day is the herald of a sunset. Earth is not our permanent home.
- The dead keep their link with the living through their virtuous deeds.

- How do Sikhs think they will be remembered after death?
- Choose a quotation for each stage of life and write it in your own words.

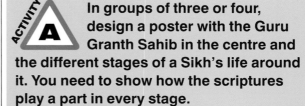

ACTIVITY **A** In groups of three or four, design a poster with the Guru Granth Sahib in the centre and the different stages of a Sikh's life around it. You need to show how the scriptures play a part in every stage.

Vaisakhi

Because Vaisakhi marks the beginning of the Sikh year, it is the time when the Nishan Sahib is replaced. Most of the community attend when the pole is taken down and the flag and the covering round the pole is removed. Everyone reaches forward to try and take part in washing the flagpole. The white substance used is natural yoghurt. This is because yoghurt is considered a gentle cleansing agent. After this is washed off and the pole dried, a new covering is put on and the new flag raised. Flag and covering are given by members of the congregation.

What does Vaisakhi celebrate?

Vaisakhi is one of the major religious festivals for Sikhs because it celebrates the founding of the Khalsa in 1699. The last human guru, Guru Gobind (he took the name Singh after this event) went to Anandpur and set up camp. He asked for five volunteers who were prepared to give their lives up for God. Eventually five brave men came forward expecting to die but instead were rewarded for their bravery when the Guru made them into his five special followers, the Panj Piare. He initiated them into this group with a ceremony called amrit sanskar. The Guru stirred water with sugar with his khanda and all of them shared the holy drink. Thereafter the five were given special clothes, the 5Ks, the name Singh (meaning 'lion') and a code of conduct. The Guru shared all of these with the Panj Piare. Later, women underwent the ceremony.

Another more sombre event is also remembered at this time. In 1919, 379 Sikhs were massacred and 2000 injured when a British general ordered his troops to fire on a Sikh crowd at Amritsar.

The Sikh new year is also celebrated at Vaisakhi and takes place on 13 or 14 April.

What happens at Vaisakhi today?

- A service begins in the Prayer Hall soon after dawn and people come in for part of it. There are readings from the Guru Granth Sahib and from poems which remind people of the first Vaisakhi. During the day there are also lectures and talks encouraging people to take amrit. The langar cooks and serves food all day long as families and friends join together to share a meal there.

- Vaisakhi is a favourite time for the amrit ceremony. This is the ceremony for Sikhs who want to become members of the Khalsa today, in other words, become baptised Sikhs. This ceremony will take place during the day in a room at the gurdwara in the presence of other members of the Khalsa.

- Outside the front of the gurdwara the community gathers to replace the Nishan Sahib with a new one.

- Street processions are very popular. The Guru Granth Sahib is at the heart of the procession, carried on a float with a Sikh reading aloud during the procession. Music and dancing, as well as other floats, accompany the scriptures.

- Vaisakhi is a time for sending cards to family and friends.

This huge decorated float carries the Guru Granth Sahib. Notice that most people who are watching on the street have their heads covered as a sign of respect. Inside the float the book rests on a manji sahib supported by cushions as it would in the gurdwara. A reader sits behind it reading. This procession with the holy book is called nagar kirtan.

- The amrit ceremony today takes place in private amongst those who have already been initiated. What are the advantages of a private ceremony over a public one?

- For discussion: Do you think that asking some people to give up their lives for their beliefs is the best way of testing how committed they are? What other ways could you think of?

- Research the code of conduct expected of Khalsa members today. Which parts of this code would you find the hardest to keep?

When is the Sikh new year and how is it celebrated?

ACTIVITY

A Use a large yellow or orange sheet of paper, cut into the shape of the Nishan Sahib as the basis of a poster about Vaisakhi. It might be a good idea to draw the Khanda symbol in the centre and work the rest of your ideas around it.

Gurpurbs and melas

Sikhs have two main sorts of festivals, gurpurbs and melas.

Although the word gurpurb might look strange, you can probably identify where the first part of the word comes from. 'Guru' means teacher and 'purb' means holiday. The two words are combined to mean a festival that celebrates an event in the life of one of the gurus. The main events which are celebrated in Britain are the birthdays of Guru Nanak and of Guru Gobind Singh. Two other more sombre events that are celebrated are the martyrdom of Guru Arjan and the martyrdom of Guru Tegh Bahadur.

Celebrating a gurpurb

Congregational worship at the gurdwara is at the core of the celebrations. A continuous reading of the Guru Granth Sahib begins at the gurdwara almost 48 hours before the festival so that the final reading will be completed on the day itself.

Another copy of Guru Granth Sahib will be installed on a float like the ones shown on page 125. This will form the main part of a street procession and the day may end with a communal fireworks display.

Fireworks are a popular part of most Sikh festivals. What do you think the light might symbolise?

Divali

Divali festival is enormously popular throughout India. It is a mela, which means a festival or celebration. The term jore melal means a time for getting together, and is used of the festivals Vaisakhi, Divali and Hola Mohalla. Divali started off as a Hindu festival that takes place in the autumn and commemorates the story of Rama and Sita in the Hindu religion. Sikhs use Divali to remember an event in their history concerning the most popular Sixth guru, Guru Hargobind.

In 1619 Guru Hargobind and 52 Hindu princes were imprisoned by the Moghul Emperor Jehangir on charges of treason. Shortly before the festival of Divali, the Emperor decided that Guru Hargobind was innocent and agreed to release him. The Guru said he would only leave if all 52 princes were released at the same time because they too were innocent. The Emperor agreed but set his own conditions. He said that Hargobind could take with him as many princes as he could get through the narrow gate, while they were holding on to his cloak.

The Guru solved that by having a cloak made with 52 long tassels on. All the princes held on to the cloak and walked to freedom, and the guru came to be known as Bandi Chhor or 'deliverer from prison'. Divali came to be known as Bandi Chhor Divas. On their arrival at Amritsar, fellow-Sikhs lit small clay lamps, to welcome the Guru home.

The celebration

As with other Sikh festivals, readings from the Guru Granth Sahib form the core of the celebration. Lights are often lit in the gurdwara or placed on window sills and steps outside and in the home.

Those Sikhs who can, visit the Golden Temple at Amritsar to remember the safe return of Guru Hargobind. Decorations at the Golden Temple with electric lights are spectacular.

- Do you think it would make a festival more meaningful for believers if they went to the place where it happened? Can you think of any similar festivals in other religions where believers try to do this?

- What is the difference between a gurpurb and a mela? Which category would you put Vaisakhi in?

- What aspect of Sikh belief was Guru Hargobind putting into practice by his actions?

ACTIVITY A Use www.sikhism.org or a reference book in the library to find out how Guru Arjan and Guru Bahadur died.

1 Most Sikhs do not feel able to keep a full copy of the Guru Granth Sahib at home. How would it need to be looked after?

2 In pairs, discuss the following question: what difficulties would pupils at your school have if they followed a devout Sikh life? Consider school uniform, lunches, PE, school social events, assemblies, friendship groups, trips, festivals, the curriculum. Make notes about the points that you both raise and then write up your own account of the discussions.

3 *All people are equal in Sikhism regardless of religion, colour or gender.* What examples would a Sikh give to support this statement? Would you agree with them or would you raise counter-arguments?

4 In groups of three or four, make a model of the takht holding a copy of a book like the Guru Granth Sahib. You can use glossy material for the romala and various spare bits of tinsel and coloured foils for the decorations around the takht. If you are feeling really ambitious you could have a go at a miniature chauri.

5 This woman is performing sewa during a Sikh festival procession.
   • What does that mean?
   • Why is she doing it?

LOOKING BACK

• What do you think she might be handing to the people walking alongside the float?

GOING FORWARD

1 Research the Golden Temple at Amritsar. You could use the internet site www.sikhs.org for a virtual tour or use an encyclopaedia. In a group of three or four, make a poster about this most important of all gurdwaras. Make sure you explain how Sikhs worship there today.

2 If you log on to the site www.sikhs.org you can hear the daily prayers being sung.

3 Find out how Sikhs celebrate the festival of Bandi Chhor Divali and use ICT to produce one or more sheets of information about it. Try to import some suitable pictures to illustrate your work. One research tip is to investigate the life of Guru Hargobind to understand why this festival has special significance for Sikhs.

4 Find out some information about Bhangra dancing. Try www.sikhseek.com. How and where is it performed?

5 Design a Sikh Quiz that could be used with your class. Base it on material you have studied in this unit.